Traveling Interstate Highway 35 with God

Recognizing When God speaks

Florence Phillips

Traveling Interstate Highway 35 With God
Recognizing When God Speaks
by Florence Phillips

Printed in the United States of America

ISBN 9781619961708

www.xulonpress.com

This book is dedicated to God for taking me on this incredible journey...to the angels he sent to deliver his messages and point the way I was to go…and to the special angel who gave me his name when I reached my destination. I love you all.

ACKNOWLEDGMENTS

I could not have completed this book without the help of some very special people.

My heartfelt thanks goes to Shirley Routin for proof reading my manuscript with the thoroughness that only a school teacher could possess, and for being as diligent as an ant at a picnic in getting me to place all my commas where they needed to be. You're the best, Shirl.

Thanks to my dear friend, Polly Kreitz, for critiquing my manuscript from an author's viewpoint. Your suggestions were very helpful. I owe you a return critique when your book is ready to be published!

My gratitude goes to Jack Walton at Xulon Press, for patiently explaining your company's publication procedure and encouraging me to turn my dream into a published book. I appreciate your kindness and help.

I offer kudos to Jose Medina, also of Xulon Press, who handled the mechanics of turning my manuscript into a completed book. Your help was invaluable in leading me through the steps of internet publication and getting my manuscript ready to submit.

Most important, a special thank you goes to God for walking beside me through every step of the journey that led to my story. You are an awesome God.

Whether you turn to the right or to the left,
Your ears will hear a voice behind you, saying,
"This is the way; walk in it." — Isaiah 30:21

PROLOGUE

All five of my grown children came home for moving day. We managed to cram most of my furniture and personal belongings into the U-Haul van my two sons, Tommy and Jeff, would drive to a storage unit in Mesquite, Texas. After the van doors were shut and secured, I watched, heartbroken, as each of my offspring bade a teary-eyed goodbye to their childhood home before driving away from it for the last time. I stayed behind so I could be alone for my final walkthrough. My footsteps echoed in the emptiness as I wandered from room-to-room remembering the youthful laughter, tears of sadness and disappointment, and the clamor of our family celebrations that had taken place here. The only things remaining of that life now were the dings and scratches left by the exuberant activity of years past. Pulling out of the driveway I didn't look back.

Heading north on Interstate Highway 35 (IH-35) out of San Antonio, my Toyota pickup loaded to capacity, I was more than a little apprehensive about my future. I had just given up my home of thirty years, left behind a loving church family that had been my strong support system for just as long, and said goodbye to dear friends that I was accustomed to seeing or talking to every day. Life as I knew it was ending. In my rearview mirror, growing smaller and farther away, I watched everything familiar vanish: the neighborhood grocery, my doctor's office, my favorite shopping mall and movie theater, my youngest daughter, Vicky, and her family, and the roads I had traveled so often that they were as recognizable as the lines on my palms. At sixty-six and widowed I was, practically speaking, a homeless person. Within me, my soul's tight hold on God's shirttails mimicked the unyielding grip my hands had on the steering wheel. I was counting on Him to get me to wherever He was calling me to go.

I hadn't planned on making this journey. And I surely didn't anticipate that I would end up where I eventually did or receive the amazing surprise that waited there, but then I hadn't been expecting the news that began everything, either. It arrived in the cold of January when 2003 was just a few days old. My husband Tom and I were sitting in Wilford Hall Medical Center on Lackland Air Force Base waiting for Dr. Taylor to give us the results of Tom's tests.

"Your scan reveals multiple tumors; every area of your brain is affected," she said. Her words landed like a slap to my face.

"Am I going to die?" Tom asked.

She looked straight in his eyes and answered with a single word. "Yes."

Tom's mouth fell open and all the muscles in his face took a downward plunge, as though they were being sucked in by a sudden and mighty pull of gravity. I knew that he wanted to be told the truth but neither of us was prepared for it to be so drastic. I guess we had grown smug thinking we had won this battle six months earlier when a routine physical had revealed a tiny cancer spot on Tom's left lung. The surgeon had immediately removed the entire lung. He was so sure he got all the cancer that he saw no need to follow up with chemo or radiation. Obviously he was wrong since new tests revealed that the cancer had metastasized to Tom's remaining lung, and now had taken over his brain.

How does one act when the person you've lived with for more than forty-three years is going to be taken away forever? I guess neither of us knew because Tom and I went through the rest of that day pretending like it was no different from any other. But for two nights, all the emotions I held in reign during the days arrived, demanding acknowledgement. As the tears slipped down my cheeks, I'd turn my back to my husband and cry into my pillow so he wouldn't hear me. Tom was the kind that always fell asleep right away and slept through everything. I assumed that hadn't changed, until night three when I rolled over and wrapped my arm around his waist. That's when I felt it against my cheek: the wet spot on his pillow. He had been crying, too.

He hugged me tightly and said, "I'm going to tell you I love you every night until I die." Tom wasn't into sentiment; he preferred not to talk about affectionate feelings so this promise was big—with a capital "B." I was deeply touched by his gift. I also felt sadness for the regret I heard in his voice for all the lost opportunities when he hadn't said the *love* word and too little time he had left to make up for it.

He was placed on hospice care at home and in less than three months—on April 19, 2003, the day after our forty-forth wedding anniversary—he breathed his last breath. I thought I had done all my mourning during his hospice care days; the loss of his hair, his appetite, his body mass, his bowel control, his dignity, his ability to walk, his consciousness. Each one was an agonizing process. So by the time he died, I didn't think I had any tears left. I felt only relief that the suffering was over.

Sitting with the crowd gathered under a canopy at Tom's burial site on Fort Sam Houston National Cemetery where he was being buried with full military honors, I watched seven military men in full dress uniform approach to honor one of their own. Their steps were respectfully slow and crisp, their shoulders back, their eyes straight ahead, their expressions, somber. They formed a perfect line, raised their rifles and shot three volleys into the air in a twenty-one gun salute. A bugler began playing "Taps" and I discovered I still had some tears left. They were silently working their way down my face, as the familiar words of the song wove through my memory: *Day is done, Gone the sun, From the lakes, From the hills, From the sky, All is well, safely rest, God is nigh*. From his seat behind me, my son Jeff tapped me on the shoulder and handed me a tissue to dry my tears. Somewhere in the distance, another bugler returned a haunting response. *Thanks and Praise, For our days, Neath the sun, Neath the stars, Neath the sky, As we go, This we know, God is nigh*. Then the airmen approached Tom's casket and in practiced precision, they folded the flag that was draped over it into a tight triangle. One of the men carried it to my chair and dropped on one knee before me while he laid the flag in my arms. I don't know if it was my tears or his own emotions that made his eyes moist as he stared directly into mine and said, "On behalf of the President of the United States, the Department of the Air Force, and a grateful nation, we offer this flag for the faithful and dedicated service of MSgt. Baurys. God bless you and this family, and God bless the United States of America." He rose and joined his entourage, and as they marched back to their vehicles, the crowd began breaking up. Vicky's husband, Steve, who is also a military career man, hurried over to the empty shells lying in the grass and picked up three of them. He brought them to me and tucked them securely into a corner of the folded flag. "These are supposed to be kept in there," he said. Three discharged shells to represent the trinity: God the Father, Son, and Holy Ghost, part of the Air Force burial tradition.

The funeral director took me by the elbow to lead me to his waiting limousine. "Wait," I said.

"We have to go now," he answered softly.

Ignoring him, I walked to Tom's casket and he followed me. "The last salute is mine," I said, then raised my right hand to my brow and saluted the man lying inside.

After the funeral, the children and grandchildren returned home to their jobs and school. I was left alone for the first time in my life.

What follows is not a pitiful account of my husband's dying; it's about me living. My story is about the lessons I learned and the joyous miracles I encountered as I journeyed solo into God's will for my life. It's about experiencing the true awesomeness of God, finding His angels in the most unexpected places, and giving to Him, completely, all that I am and all that I would become. Mostly, it's about hearing—with absolute certainty—God speaking to me and the many ways I heard his voice. My story is one I need to share…with you.

1

S uddenly, I found myself in a whole new world—the world of widowhood. I thought I was prepared for it but I actually knew nothing about this life. It had been a long time since I was totally on my own, and I was a lot younger then. I left my parents' home at age eighteen to move into the dorm at nursing school where I had "house mothers" and strict rules to follow. In my senior year, I married a military man and after graduation I followed him from one duty assignment to another; the birth of our children followed. Now that Tom had died and my children were out on their own, I was alone again. There were moments when I reveled in the freedom to do whatever I pleased; other times I wasn't sure how to fill the loneliness. Sometimes I felt adventuresome and explored new places and things; sometimes I just wanted to be at home in my comfort zone. At moments I felt very capable of taking care of business; other moments I felt confused and hesitant. Getting oriented to widowhood and being a single homeowner was definitely a challenge. I'm sure this scary, uneasy feeling is common to all people when the realty of losing a spouse sets in. It wasn't that I was afraid of this life change. I had done all kinds of things on my own when I was a military wife and Tom went on temporary duty to another location or was sent on a permanent change of station where he'd be gone for a year. Keeping up the house and caring for five very young children by myself, I learned that I could do whatever I had to. Now, I didn't have children to think about; it was just me. The pressure I was feeling came from having so many things to do right away.

For instance, Tom's death brought on mountains of paperwork necessary to settle the legalities and finances of our estate—a chore that was at the least, exhausting, and ultimately, daunting. I had to get copies of his Death Certificate made and go before a judge to acquire Letters of Testament in order to show I now had full right to all of our belongings in case I needed to sell anything. The insurance company needed to be notified of his death, as did the Office of Personnel Management where his annuity checks came from. Tom was not into organization; all of his personal paperwork (some of which I needed to accomplish my tasks) was stuffed into a large trash bag, along with papers of no significance. I had to go through it piece-by-piece to be sure I didn't throw away anything important.

All this paperwork required time, locating offices, legwork, and phone calls which often resulted in being transferred from person to person or being "on hold" for way too long. As fate would have it, some things didn't go smoothly. Tom had worked a civil service job after finishing his military career, and when I notified the personnel office of his death they immediately stopped his monthly annuity. They seemed to be dragging their feet, though, in starting my survivor benefit checks. I had no money coming in and I wasn't sure how much I'd get once my checks started to arrive. He had only a very small life insurance policy, and raising five children on an enlisted man's pay didn't leave us with much money to build up a sizeable savings. I was worried about my financial situation.

Keeping up the yard work was another nuisance to be dealt with. The back yard pool required frequent cleaning, chemical testing, and balancing. It was a gift from a much loved uncle who left me some money when he died. We decided to install the pool with the money so all members of our large family could benefit from the gift. Children, grandchildren, and friends had celebrated many happy occasions here, barbecuing, playing water games, sunning on lounge chairs. But after cancer came to live with us, the pool was ignored. Even though it wasn't being used, I had to maintain it to keep algae from growing on the surface and causing trouble. Then there were the flower beds that Tom had planted. He loved gardening; I didn't. And the big pecan tree needed seasonal harvesting and spraying against webworms. One of my more difficult tasks was sorting through Tom's fishing and golf equipment and clothing, then packing it up and recycling it to various organizations. Dealing with his personal belongings was a very emotional thing. It felt like every piece I gave away was a piece of him being disposed of.

Of course, I gave the children a chance to take whatever they wanted. Though we had raised them all the same, they all turned out differently and had their own personalities and interests (which, I'm sure was God's plan) so it was interesting to me to see what each one chose to keep. Lori, who is talented in arts and crafts, wanted his fishing lures to decorate her Christmas tree; a part of him would be with her through every Christmas season. Jeff, a golfer, took some of Tom's golf shirts, hoping that having something of his dad's on the golf course would bring him good luck. He also wanted a Bible that was presented to his dad. Vicky wanted his Air Force dress uniform. She and her husband wanted to own a coffee shop for veterans one day—a place where military retirees could drink strong coffee and swap stories, where they could discuss politics and world problems—which were what old sergeants do. Military uniforms and memorabilia would be hung on the walls of their shop. Tommy, was happy to have Tom's Smoky Bear hat—a special hat worn by those who train raw recruits when they enter the military, a hat that speaks of toughness and rules, of learning teamwork and watching each other's backs so they could care for one another should they find themselves in a war zone (This son has been through a few personal wars of his own). Wendy, the remaining daughter didn't want anything special but she accepted one of her dad's commendation medals—an award given for outstanding performance. She has endured way too many health issues and surgeries, plus dealing with deep family heartaches, including raising a bipolar child. If anyone deserved to share in her dad's award, it was she. Her husband, who is always tinkering with vehicles or old lawnmowers, took Tom's tools.

Though all this work and upheaval was exhausting, establishing order in my life again was all part of recovery for me; it was something that I, personally, had to do in order to move on. The reason I am including it in my story is to shed some light for others on how they can help people they know who have lost a spouse. Friends and family are so supportive and loving when a loved one dies but after the funeral they seem to disappear. The best thing they can do is take the survivor out of the house for a short event or activity so they can put their troubles aside for awhile. Notice I said *short*. Too long away from home keeps them from doing what they have to do. One of the greatest gifts I received during my adjustment period was an invitation from my daughter Vicky to go out to lunch with her and her friend Maria. I quickly accepted, glad for a break from my chores. I knew Maria only vaguely. Her husband, who had also served in the Air Force, died six months before Tom. Since she had already experienced the aftermath of becoming a military widow, Vicky thought Maria might be able to answer my questions and give me some direction in getting things done. Over lunch in a beautiful restaurant with a glass wall that looked out over lush woods and flower gardens, I felt my body relax and absorb the serenity. The three of us fell easily into girl-talk before moving on to more serious topics like how we felt after our losses, the changes our lives had taken, and the government's slow response in settling my claim. It was a wonderful afternoon yet I was back home in two hours and able to finish my to-do list for the day. Spending some time with these two women was a perfect way to help me feel refreshed and know others were thinking of me.

What I did not expect was something that happened just before we left the restaurant. Please understand that I am not suggesting this should be part of your day out with others. I was fortunate to receive an extra blessing from our luncheon, one I can only define as a wake-up call from God. When we had finished eating, Maria pulled her checkbook from her purse and began filling out a check. I assumed she was going to use it to pay for her lunch. Instead, she slid it across the table to me. "Use this while you're waiting for your checks to arrive," she said.

I was astounded when I saw the amount of two thousand dollars on the check written out to me. "Oh, thank you, but I can't take this. I'll be okay," I assured her.

"Take it," she said, pushing it back in my direction. "If you don't need it, you can give it back, but if you find you need it, spend it."

I had never received such a generous offer, especially from someone I barely knew. Her kindness and generosity stunned me but at the same time it eased my mind to know I had the money at hand if I got desperate enough to borrow some of it. As it turned out, several weeks after our luncheon, the first of my monthly checks arrived, an amount sufficient to meet all my financial needs. With huge gratitude, I returned Maria's un-cashed check. On contemplating this event I saw that Maria's compassionate act was God's way of telling me that I did not have to worry about money or anything else; He would take care of all my needs, just as it says in the Bible: *"And my God will meet all your needs according to his glorious riches in Christ Jesus."* (Philippians 4:19)

A friend once asked me during a Bible study we were attending, "How do you know when God is speaking to you? I've never heard Him speak."

I didn't know how to answer her. I've known at times that God was speaking to me; I just didn't know how to explain it. Now that I was alone, I was spending more quiet time reading scripture and praying. Maybe that was teaching me to listen better or perhaps I was beginning to acquire a clearer understanding of divine communication. Obviously it's no booming voice coming from heaven. It's receiving clear insight of what God is telling me, and knowing unmistakably that it is He speaking. I firmly believe that He uses human voices and acts to deliver messages from Him. Some of the messengers are strangers; others are people I know well. Since they are serving God's purpose in this way, I call them His angels. Maria was the first God-sent angel, the beginning step in a journey with God I had yet to learn was going to happen.

One way God speaks is through earthly angels.

While I was busy with my chores, I was completely unaware of the vultures circling outside my home. In our neighborhood, the mailboxes are placed along the curb; they sit atop a post fixed in the ground, two boxes to a post every other house. Mine was on the same post as my next-door neighbor to my right. One day, shortly after Tom's burial, I went out to check mail and my neighbor showed up at the same time. Without hesitation, he asked me to go out with him. I was totally unprepared for an invitation like this so soon after my husband's death. Dating was definitely not on my mind. I refused his invitation but every time I went to check my mail this guy showed up and asked me out again. It wasn't just his bad timing that turned me off; our families had never been on friendly terms. His teenage son was a gang member and had caused numerous problems for us, including burglarizing our home and taking hundreds of dollars worth of our posses-sions. We never got any of it back, nor an apology, or any effort on the parents' part to make amends. Now the son was in prison and the rest of the family had all gone their separate ways, except for the dad who still lived in the house and spent his evenings in a bar—too much bad history for him and me to become friends, even if I was interested which, as I said, I was not. Thankfully, after several refusals, he stopped asking me out.

Then vulture number two made his appearance. Tom's friend, who lived two doors up on the other side of my house, came to see me one day, wanting to know if I was doing okay and if I needed help with anything. We were talking through the screen door when suddenly he pulled it open and stepped inside. Grabbing me in a bear hug, he planted a hard kiss on my lips. This could have been a serious situation. He was a big man and very obese; I was no match to his strength. I don't know how I got this character back out the door; I can only believe that God had my back covered. After that, I kept my doors locked and before going out to check mail or get in my car, I always looked out the windows to make sure neither of these men was around. But one day I was doing some work in the back yard. The only way to see into my back yard from the street out front was through a small gate at a sidewalk that led along the side of the house. Feeling secure, I guess I let my guard down. Tom's friend suddenly appeared beside me. He tried to get me into our woodworking shop, wearing an evil smile that suggested it would be fun. I made it clear to him that was not going to happen and walked him back to the gate to be sure he left. I was annoyed with myself for not being more aggressive right from the first encounter but I never saw it coming. When it did, I was too shocked to think straight. Now he was back and I didn't say or do anything to encourage his visit. I was really angry and called to talk to Vicky since she was the only one of my family living in town. She encouraged me to have the police serve him with papers to keep him from entering my property. Only one thing stopped me from doing that, his wife. She was a sweet woman who had visited Tom with her husband while he was fighting cancer. I didn't think she knew what her husband was up to and I didn't want to hurt her. I decided to give it more time and see if the creep wised up. Days passed and he did not come back; I hoped I had seen the last of him.

If this happened to me, it was happening to other new widows. We need to speak out about this problem. It needs to be brought out in the open so it can be dealt with and punished or resolved. I didn't tell my other children what had happened, but I was aware that they were worried about me living alone. "Move closer to us so we can help you," urged Jeff.

"You can stay with us," said Lori. "With Christi away at college and no one using her room, you can have it all to yourself."

Vicky voiced her opinion, too. "I'd feel a lot better if I knew that you were close to one of my siblings when we have to leave"

She, too, was married to a career Air Force Sergeant, and they were due to be re-assigned to a different base soon, which meant they would be leaving San Antonio. I understood everyone's reasoning. With Vicky leaving and my other children already moved away and raising families in their own homes, I'd have no family nearby. Although I was healthy, active, and capable of taking care of myself, my children were too far away to get here in a hurry if I had a crisis. With my partner gone, I didn't need such a big house. There were rooms I never entered, except when they needed dusting or vacuuming. As I contemplated my situation and my children's urgings, I learned that people have very definite ideas about moving after a spouse's death. Friends, and even my sister, who lived 1800 miles away, reminded me of the so-called two-year rule. "I've heard that you should never make major changes until two years after losing your spouse," she said.

Ultimately, it was my own feelings, not the opinion of others, which had me dragging my feet over this decision. My home had many sentimental attachments; I wasn't sure I could walk away from it. For one thing, I had lived in this home for thirty years, longer than I had spent in any place since I'd been born. It's where our children grew into young adults, got their driver's licenses, started their first jobs, married, and brought grandchildren home to visit. Around this kitchen table, Tom and I had made plans, settled family crises, and celebrated life's joys. My hands, heart, and sweat left their marks on this home as I cleaned, scrubbed, and kept my family going. I had painted its walls, caulked the sinks, laid new flooring, and even installed a tile tub surround by myself. I needed the comfort of blanketing myself in the memories and familiarity of this house to get past the shock of death and change.

2

Before long, God sent another angel my way. The phone rang and when I answered, it was my grand-daughter Christi calling. She was the first born of my eight grandchildren and we were very close.

"Gram," she said, "My summer break is starting and I thought I'd come spend it with you since it's your first summer without Papa."

Christi was a college student and when she didn't have classes, she worked as a waitress to help pay her expenses. Usually, she went home to Mesquite during summer break. I didn't want to deny her time with her parents and sisters, or her friends back home. "You're so sweet, and I truly appreciate the offer but it isn't necessary. I don't want you to give up your friends and your job to be with me," I said, though I didn't really mean the words, a visit from her would be a delight.

"I already talked to my boss and he arranged for me to transfer to their restaurant in San Antonio for the summer so I could stay with you," she said.

I was thrilled to have a young girl in the house again: her energy and capacity to love were welcome gifts. We shopped from the Penney's catalog, had long heart-to-heart talks, pigged out on junk food, or ate good home-cooked meals. I was one happy Grammy! One morning she came bouncing into the kitchen early and clad in her exercise gear even though she had worked the late shift at the restaurant the night before.

"Are you ready to go walking?" she asked.

Christi knew very well that her Papa and I had walked the fitness track at the Air Force Base every morning. I understood that she was trying to get me back into the routine that was once my "normal" life so I willingly complied. After we'd done a couple laps of walking side-by-side, Christi announced, "I think I'll jog for awhile."

I am a speed walker but I don't run so I told her to go on ahead. When she was halfway around the oval track she slowed to a walk. I, too, slowed so she could catch up to me. But the slower I walked, the slower she walked. I figured something was wrong so I stopped and waited for her, and as she neared I could see the tears running down her cheeks.

"I miss Papa. I always thought when I had babies one day, he would hold them in his arms," she said. "I didn't visit him when he was sick because I couldn't face seeing him that way."

I saw how she was struggling with guilt as well as her grief and told her the truth that I hoped would ease her: "He didn't want anyone to see him after he lost so much weight and his hair fell out from chemo treatments," I told her. "It's best you remember him the way you knew him. He wanted that."

We walked one more lap arm in arm, both of us straining to keep our tears in check. There were no words for the kind of pain she felt so we just held onto each other. By the time we got back to my parked car we had both worked our way through a big chunk of healing.

Christi wanted to see where her mom had lived as a little girl when we were stationed on this base during

Papa's military career. I drove by the housing area and parked at the curb in front of the living quarters that we had been assigned to. I pointed out the bedroom window where her mom and sisters had slept, the back yard full of trees where her uncles had 'pretend wars' with their GI Joe figures, and I gave a description of the inside of the house as I recalled early years spent there. The surrounding area, however, had changed; new housing and roads had been added. It didn't look like the same neighborhood where my children had once played. For my family, nothing would ever be the same.

Having Christi with me for the summer kept my mind occupied and my heart full of joy—until the day something bad happened. As soon as she came in the door from her shift at the restaurant, I saw that she was upset. The reason for it poured from her in anxious words interspersed with tears.

"Someone stole my purse while I was working. My cell phone…my student parking permit…driver's license… my money…everything. It's all gone."

"Where was your purse?" I asked, wondering how this happened.

"Under the front seat of my pickup. I hid it under there when I went in to work. I know I locked the door. And it was still locked when I came out. But my purse was gone."

Her first impulse was to call her dad to tell him that his credit card, which he gave her to pay for school expenses, was stolen. She struggled with an onslaught of jumbled explanations as she fought to control the turmoil within her while she explained the incident to him. "There are no lockers for employees in the restaurant. What was I supposed to do with it? Yes, I locked my door!"

Apparently, the thief was someone who knew her routine and also knew how to get in and out of her pickup without being seen or leaving evidence of the break-in. I called the police as soon as she got off the phone with her dad. They came and took a report, then went to the restaurant to talk to people and look around. But they were unable to find out who did it. I felt terrible that all this happened because of the sacrifice Christi made to come and be with me. I could not let my granddaughter be at risk any longer. I had to send her back to her safe college town and the house she shared with two other students. Though she bravely protested about leaving me before summer was over, she finally gave in. I bought her a new cell phone to have in case of emergencies, and we said our good-byes. When she left, I missed her dearly, but her visit had shown me that my family needed me, and I needed them. I wasn't really alone; we were just in different places.

With Christi gone, summer half over, and all my post-funeral responsibilities settled, I was finally ready to move on with my life. Oddly, I was struck by the profound silence of the house. No little noises of another person moving about, no shower running, no toilet flushing, no talking, no sneezes, just total quiet. But the silence was my friend. I liked to open the bay window and listen to the soft melody of the waterfall cascading into the pool. It was so peaceful and calming, as was the chirping of the birds calling to one another. Writing at my computer for hours without being interrupted was a blessing, too. And since I didn't have to compete with the constant drone of the TV, I often turned on the radio to my favorite music station and danced my booty off. Weird, I know, but is weird really weird if nobody is present to see you? I love to dance. As a young girl, I lived within walking distance of a large amusement park. An open-air dance hall was located in that park, and I went there at least one night a week and stayed until closing. That stopped when I married Tom; he didn't like to dance. At our children's weddings, he'd whip me around the dance floor for one or two songs then call it quits. But that doesn't count; as the father of the bride, he was obligated to dance with the mom. The one negative thing about the silence was what it did to my voice. Sometimes I did not speak for two or three days because there was nobody around to listen. Well, I talked to God but those conversations were silent, too. When someone did show up, or the phone rang, my voice came out scratchy and hoarse from not using it, and the volume was weak. Only after I conversed for awhile did my normal voice return. I was totally surprised by this phenomenon.

In this phase of solitude, I began to rediscover the person that had been put on hold while I was wife, mother, grandmother, and great-grandma. My time and priorities for many years had been concentrated on following my military husband around two continents, serving as girl scout leader, room mom, attending little-league sports, band performances, and other family-oriented activities—which was a wonderful life—but those times were gone, and the only one I had to worry about now was me. I admit I went a little crazy checking out various places and activities and found plenty of enticements. When a friend from church told me about line-dancing lessons she was taking, I joined her and had such fun that I kept going back every week. I signed up for day-tours with a travel agency in my city. They were not only interesting and informative but a lot of fun and a great way to meet new people, especially other widows. The community college announced a class in Italian and since I had always been fascinated with the smooth sounds and rhythm of that language I jumped on the opportunity to learn it. I got so wrapped up in the lessons that I didn't even mind doing the homework.

When one activity ended there was always a new one to try. Browsing through the newspaper, I saw that a community theater was offering an acting class. After some slight hesitation, I enrolled in it. I wasn't interested in acting but the advertisement said it would help improve public speaking skills. When I published a book several years ago, I was interviewed on TV, radio, by phone, and in the newspaper. I was also hired to speak to various groups of adults or children, all of which was a challenge for me. I hoped the acting class would help me be more at ease and do a better job of speaking professionally. After I got into it, I found out that acting was definitely not my forté, but I enjoyed being with the other students. It was fun for the eight weeks that it lasted and doing a performance for friends and family on our final night. All of these endeavors nourished my soul and brought happiness and new knowledge to my life.

While I was busy rediscovering myself, summer slipped away and colder temperatures arrived. I had fun doing Halloween with Vicky and her daughter Sydnie, and I also had Thanksgiving dinner at their house. But with the Christmas holidays approaching I found myself feeling melancholy and uneasy about experiencing the most celebrated Christian event in the calendar year without my partner. I'd heard from others how holidays, anniversaries, and birthdays after losing a spouse are difficult. They were right. Even though I felt like I was enjoying the freedom to do as I pleased, I was not ready to face Christmas alone. With so many children and grandchildren, this holiday was always a big time for our family. After some contemplation I made up my mind to drive to the Dallas area, where three of my grown children and their families lived; that would put me in contact with the largest part of my family. I dove into shopping for gifts and baking so I'd have plenty of home-baked Christmas goodies to take with me.

My plans, however, hit a snag when I got a crisis call from Charles Posey, an old friend and retired Air Force Chaplain who attended the same church I did. Though he was no longer actively preaching he continued to look after the sick and needy people in our congregation. He was calling to tell me that one of the men was rushed to the hospital and was in surgery getting a pacemaker. His wife Helen was diabetic and had never given her own insulin injections—that was her husband's task.

"Since you were a nurse at one time, I thought you might help her out while he is in the hospital," he said.

"I'm getting ready to go out of town for the holidays," I said. "But I'd be glad to give her injections until I have to leave."

She needed one in the morning and another at bedtime, around 10:00 PM. I was not comfortable about going out after dark, especially since I did not know my way around her neighborhood. Gang presence and crime had been growing steadily in our area. Still, I couldn't let her down. I knew Helen from seeing her at church, though not on a personal level. During my twice-a-day visits, I'd linger awhile so we could talk, and I was getting to know her better. I was worried about what she would do if her husband didn't make it or if another crisis came up and there was no one around who could help her. I decided to teach Helen how to give the shots to herself. On my next visit I took an orange with me. As I prepared to give her insulin, I explained every step from measuring the dose and watching for air bubbles in the syringe to cleaning and injecting her skin. When I was done, I told her to wash out the syringe and needle and use it to practice injecting water into the orange so she could get the feel of it. But each time I visited, she wasn't ready to give the shot herself. Soon it was time for me to leave on my trip. Ready or not, Helen was on her own and I was on my way out of town. But just in case she couldn't handle it, Charles had found another nurse who would fill in if she was needed.

My first stop was Jeff's house. Tommy lived with him so I had the bonus of being able to make merry with both sons together. When I arrived, Jeff's two children ran to meet me and immediately started showing me all the gifts already under the tree. The house was beautifully decorated and alive with excitement. I knew right away that coming here for the holidays was the right thing to do.

On Christmas Eve, Jeff's wife, who is Catholic, wanted to go to Midnight Mass. Since I am Methodist they gave me a choice to opt out but I chose to go with them. The order and style of worship was totally unfamiliar and I couldn't understand a single word of the message delivered in Latin, but a moment came when I felt myself being drawn into that mystical feeling of wonder associated with the Baby Jesus' birth. When it happened, God's spirit was almost visible to me. Even though I was hearing the Christmas story with new words, the message came into my heart and soul with perfect understanding, just as it does in my English-speaking church service every Christmas Eve.

God speaks in many languages — and gives us understanding.

What a joy for me to wake the next morning surrounded by family. My grandchildren's squeals of delight and excitement nearly blew out the windows as they tore open their gifts, burying the floor with remnants of wrapping paper. I had almost forgotten the energy of children discovering Santa's gifts, and there were plenty to discover under this tree. Watching my grandchildren made me think about those long-ago years when my kids were little, when their dad's meager enlisted man's pay and our large family was not an easy mix. But I always tried to make Christmas fun for them. One year in particular came to my mind. I had collected empty grocery store cartons—one for each child—and placed their gifts inside. Then using an assortment of brightly colored paper, magic markers, empty paper towel rolls and other odds and ends, I created a building from each box: a sparkly castle, a barber shop, a school complete with bell tower, etc. The boxes helped make gift-opening more special and the gifts inside seem like more than they were. On Christmas morning the children were delighted. As it turned out, the boxes caused as much excitement as the gifts—maybe even more. They played with them all that day and for days after, until the boxes were tattered and torn. Our status back then did not compare to what Jeff's children were experiencing but the excitement and love was the same. Life is an ongoing endeavor and God is the constant that gets us through.

My grandchildren weren't the only ones who got spoiled that morning. Though I knew they missed their dad, my sons and daughter-in-law showered me with gifts and attention to make my Christmas special and keep me from missing Tom. I know that special days will always be difficult times, but I'm prepared to deal with it. It's a miniscule thing in comparison to the blessings I've been given. After we had eaten the scrumptious breakfast that Tommy and Jeff whipped up, I left for Lori's house to have Christmas with her family.

A plethora of mouth-watering smells wafted out to meet me as I walked up the front sidewalk. My daughter is an excellent cook, which she doesn't get from her mom. Inside, the scene was the same as what I left at Jeff's house—times three. Two pets added to the mayhem here. The cat was getting into everything it should not be doing, and their big lummox of a dog—a mixed breed who thinks he's of the human genre—paraded around in a nervous dither. After dinner and extra desserts—that were eaten through fake protests—we played board games, a passion in my family that has been passed on to the younger generation and which gets noisier as the competition heats up. With all the talk and laughter, the dog was now wearing an expression that said *this is my domain, why doesn't everybody get out?* For a fleeting moment I thought about taking him up on it, silently stealing away to return to my quiet existence in San Antonio. But to be truthful, I loved the madness of a happy, healthy family living life as it should be. Christmas reigned at the Shelton home, and I soaked it all up like stale bread in a bowl of milk. My holidays had been everything a family celebration should be. I would have been bogged down in loneliness without their kind attentions and the bubbly energy of grandkids to distract me. Instead, I fell into bed that night feeling saturated with the love of family, the goodness of God, and gratitude for the Christ child who gave us this reason for celebrating.

With the New Year just a week away, I contemplated on what had been quite a year for me. Lying here with the wonder of Christmas in my heart, I felt like the upheaval following Tom's death was behind me. Maybe now my life could settle into some form of order and predictability. I wondered what 2004 would bring.

On the first Sunday after I returned home, I went to the worship service at church and was taken by surprise with the greeting I received. Helen and her husband, who was doing very well with his pacemaker, met me with enthusiastic hugs and smiles. Her voice was bubbling with joy when she announced that she was giving her own injections. Both of them kept thanking me for what I'd done and said I was their angel, which is how they continued to refer to me from then on. I had dreaded going out after dark to give Helen her evening dose of insulin but I'm glad I didn't give in to my fear. This experience showed me how God can take my apprehensions about serving others and turn them into blessings when I'm willing to serve Him. In addition to learning a lesson, my small act brought me two special friends. And Helen's courage in using the knowledge I shared with her would benefit the rest of her life. This was my best Christmas gift.

3

We were only several months into the New Year when I awoke one morning knowing it was time to move out of the house. I felt it as certain as if the message had descended straight from the lips of God and had bedded down in my subconscious waiting for me to waken and find it. It grew like a quiet stirring deep within me that would not let me go until I acknowledged it. I have had these episodes before. I'm sure others have experienced them, too. For example, I will suddenly get thoughts of one of my children, and the urgency feels so strong that I have to stop and pray for him/her even though I don't know exactly what I'm praying for. Later, I'll learn that they were experiencing a bad time or some sort of hazard at that moment. Or I may have nagging thoughts about granddaughter Christi at college, so I'll write her a note and tuck some money inside. A few days later, she'll call full of thanks because she received the money at a time when she had an unexpected expense at school and needed help. I choose to call this phenomenon *heart whispers*.

God speaks through heart whispers.

The heart whisper I received this morning was alive and unquestionable in my mind, a feeling so strong that I didn't have to give it more thought. I knew without a doubt that God was telling me to leave this house. I had no idea what would happen or where I was to go but I was absolutely certain that He wanted me to follow where He led me. Having acknowledged the feeling and the certainty of it, I was ready to act on it. I began by looking for a realtor to sell my house. A few days into the task, I received a phone call from Charles Posey. What he had to say further convinced me that God was calling me to follow Him.

"I didn't want to say anything until you made a decision to sell your house," said Charles. "Now that you have, I'd like to give you the name and phone number of Dave Harvey. He's a Christian realtor who helped another member of our church sell her home after her husband died. Dave did a good job for her and I think he'll be fair with you."

I had call waiting and while we were talking my other line beeped. Having finished what he wanted to tell me, Charles said a hurried goodbye so I could answer the incoming call.

"This is Dave Harvey," said the voice on the other end of the line. I was so stunned upon hearing the name that Charles just referred to me that all I could do was listen.

"I sold a house for a woman from your church two years ago and for some reason I had an urge to call her this morning and see how she was doing. She told me about your situation and said you're trying to sell your house. I thought I might be of some help."

Of course I agreed to meet with him. The way I see it, when Dave called the woman from my church after two years of being out of touch with her, he was acting on similar heart whispers as I had experienced on awaking a few days earlier. Then God used her as His angel to send Dave to me. At the same time this was happening, God was working on Charles to introduce me to Dave's name and reputation so I'd know I could trust him. All of this had to be part of God's plan for me. There's no way I can accept that all of these people came together with the same thought at the same time merely by coincidence.

God speaks through more heart whispers, more angels.

I liked Dave so we signed a contract. We discussed the fact that my house might not sell very fast because of the way the neighborhood had deteriorated and gang activity arrived. There was also concern about the improvements we made during the thirty years we lived here which raised the value of the house beyond others in the neighborhood. When we moved in, this was a delightful area and our house compared to all others on the street. But over time we made many changes to accommodate our growing family. We converted the garage into another bedroom with a bay window; and we did a major update on the kitchen. Our biggest change, a fifteen by thirty family room added to the back of the house, was accompanied by a large covered patio. And we installed the pool in the back yard. We also erected the outbuilding that housed a woodworking shop and storage for yard tools. While all this made a cozy nest for our family of seven, I probably would not get what it was worth when I sold it. People don't like to buy an attractive house in a neighborhood that is falling apart, even when the lot is fenced in, as ours was. Considering all this, I worried about the cash outcome. I know what you're thinking, and you're right; I had given my money worries to God after he sent Maria to me. Now I was trying to take them back. So, tightening my faith around me like a battle shield, I moved forward, confident that selling the house was what God wanted me to do.

I began sorting through the "stuff" that acquires with thirty years of living in one place. My heartstrings tugged painfully as I unwillingly parted with souvenirs from our Air Force travels, woodwork items made by my husband's hands, and other belongings that wouldn't fit into a down-sized home. I am one of those sentimental people that have trouble parting with things that have special meaning rather than for their monetary value. But the change in my life situation made me see everything in a different way. I assume other widows and widowers eventually reach that point, too. But often it takes time to get to there. I had to be practical now, and forget about keeping things that weren't essential for my future existence. I also needed to sell one of our vehicles—something I'd been procrastinating about since Tom's death. My Saturn was paid off and was in excellent condition. Financially, it would have been the best vehicle to keep, but Tom's Toyota pickup would be much more useful for the work ahead of me. It took several weeks to find a buyer for the Saturn and I had to take less than I asked for it but at least I had one less worry. Finally, with all my packed boxes moved into one room, Dave hung the "For Sale" sign in my front yard. I hoped I'd at least get enough for a down payment on another home. If not, I was in deep trouble.

Unfortunately, the sale sign brought trouble I was not expecting. Tom's friend showed up again and he was all emotional. "You can't move," he said. "What am I going to do without you?"

Listening to him made me realize how out of touch with reality he was. I didn't fear him on this visit; I pitied him. I also assured him that I was looking forward to my move and happy to be leaving this area. Thankfully, he left without pushing the subject any further.

Miraculously, two days after the sign was hung, Dave called to say we had a serious offer from a buyer. I was shocked by the quick response. They, however, wanted me to pay all closing costs, cutting my share of the sale quite a bit. I was not happy about this and questioned Dave about it.

"If you don't accept this offer, it may take six or more months to find another buyer interested in living in this area," he said. "So what do you want me to do?"

I didn't want to risk waiting that long. God was calling and I was anxious to find out what He had in store for me so I agreed to pay closing costs. Then I learned that the buyers wanted to move in by the end of the month, giving me only two weeks to get out. I was counting on having more time to sell the furniture that I didn't want to take with me. And I still hadn't cleared out the building in the backyard, which was full of hand tools, table saws, hardware and lumber pieces from our days of making home furnishings and knick-knacks that we sold in local outlets. Once more, I felt a ton of pressure on my shoulders wondering how I'd get everything done in two weeks. Fortunately, my children and their spouses took on some of the chores. I was beyond sentimentality now; I gave stuff away and threw things out without worrying about it. Lori came from Mesquite and spent a weekend clearing out my kitchen. I hadn't boxed any of that stuff yet because I was still cooking and eating at home. She even put all of it in her SUV and took it home with her to store in her garage, leaving more room for my furniture in the U-Haul truck. Tommy and Jeff were going to pick up my household goods and said they'd take all the furniture and put it in storage. I could sell what I didn't need when I got to my next house. Another crisis solved! God, it seemed, was determined to get me going.

With the same reasoning that I used to decide to go to north Texas for Christmas, I figured my best option for a new home would be the Dallas area where Lori and my sons were located. It seemed as good a starting place as any for God to lead me wherever He wanted me to be. Vicky's husband was still expecting to get relocation orders, leaving Wendy—the only family member I'd have left in this part of Texas. I love Wendy as much as the other children, but she lived about 50 miles south of San Antonio in a rural area trailer park. I knew I wouldn't be happy there without the conveniences of city living. Also, she worked full time so I wouldn't see her much. I decided that I would take up the offer of Lori and her husband to stay with them in Christi's room while I looked for a place of my own. I must admit, I was nervous about the drive. The Toyota pickup was in excellent condition but it normally was not used for hauling heavy loads, and on moving day it was packed to capacity with items I wanted to keep with me and not put into storage. The hours dwindled by, as I stared into the miles of pavement before me. I prayed frequently, thanking God for bringing me safely this far and asking that He stay close for the rest of the journey. And I had discussions with Him about what He had in store for me up ahead. I wanted to be sure He knew I was putting my trust and my life in His hands and was willing to go where He led me. I could think of no other choice I would make at this time. To combat the loneliness of not having another voice in the truck, I didn't hesitate to pray out loud at times—or sing along with the CDs I had put within easy reach on the front seat. I can only imagine what people in the passing traffic were thinking. Picture a gray-haired lady driving a loaded-down pickup along the busy corridor of IH-35, and talking to an obviously empty seat beside her. The Beverly Hillbillies comes quickly to my mind.

I considered myself to be physically fit; I eat well, keep my weight down, get enough sleep, and speed walk every morning. But age evidently was proving to me that I couldn't handle the arduous challenges, like preparing for a three-hundred-mile relocation, the way I usually breezed through things. By the time I pulled into the driveway at Lori's house I was physically and emotionally exhausted, which probably explains the horrible upper respiratory infection I contacted. I quickly learned that some doctors won't accept new Medicare patients. When I found one that did, he didn't help me much. A racking cough kept me awake nights, and I felt so weak that I couldn't sit up for long. I wanted to go to bed and sleep for the next six months. I'd just begun an adventure into a new life and I already missed the Air Force doctors that had provided my care for the last forty-five years. I was desperate for relief when I learned of a community clinic not far from Lori's house. Here, I found a more caring doctor who diagnosed bronchitis and prescribed medication that helped a lot, though the nagging cough lingered for several weeks. Following God, even though I was confident it was what

He wanted, was already proving to be difficult—and this was just the beginning of a journey with my Lord.

Whether I was stubborn or determined depends on who was making the call because every day that I felt strong enough, I went house hunting with the real estate agent I had hired. Melba was a blessing, treating me as kindly as if I were her own mother, even worrying about my lingering cough. She exhibited extreme patience and was dedicated to finding exactly what I wanted in a house. She drove endless miles so we could check out houses for sale, not only in Grand Prairie where I'd be close to my boys, and Mesquite where Lori lives, but throughout nearby towns all along Highway 20. There were days when we checked out as many as fifteen houses. But Melba never gave up on me. I didn't find this caring person by coincidence; I would not have known to contact the real-estate company where she worked if it hadn't been for an old friend. Finding Melba was another one of my "Aha" moments.

Before leaving San Antonio, my friend gave me the name of a Real Estate Company. "When you get to where you're going, look them up," he said.

"Have you used them before?" I asked.

"No, but I was a realtor before I met your family. Word gets around in the business. This company has a good record and a reputation for treating their clients well."

I did as he said, and that's how Melba came into my life.

God speaks through angels.

When we first started the house hunt, I told Melba that I would like to be halfway between Lori and my sons so I could get to either of their homes easily.

"I think you'll have to decide on one or the other," she said. "I wouldn't feel right putting you in the area midway between them. There are too many slums and questionable neighborhoods in that vicinity."

Because of her knowledge of this part of Texas, I decided to go with the options she thought would be safe for a single senior female living alone. Weeks dragged into one month, then another. Everything we looked at was either too expensive or needed too many repairs. I no longer had a helpmate or the funds to hire someone to do major work. The fruitless house hunting left me frustrated, and I became discouraged with my unhinged situation. I had not planned on it taking so long to find a home.

Living out of a suitcase was becoming a nightmare, too. I knew my limited wardrobe was obvious to others when I came downstairs one morning and met up with my granddaughter Rebekah at the bottom step.

"Grammy," she said, with an exasperated sigh, "Why do you always wear the same colors?"

She could not understand that the old house in San Antonio that she'd been visiting since she was born no longer belonged to Grammy and Papa, and that I just couldn't go and get more of my clothes. My storage shed was crammed so tightly that there was no way I could get in there and move things around to find other clothing or anything else. I had to keep washing and re-wearing what was packed in my one big suitcase. To make matters worse, when I'd forget to close my suitcase or shut the bedroom door, the family cat would make a bed in my clothes. Everything I wore was embellished with cat-hair designs.

Clothing wasn't the only problem. I still had monthly bills to pay, which meant payment books and bank accounts to keep track of, not to mention the hordes of paperwork I had acquired both from the sale of my home in San Antonio and information on houses I was looking at in this area. I missed my computer which was in storage and would have been a lot of help. Though I was normally a very organized person, I could no longer keep track of the things I stuffed into paper bags and boxes while living in one bedroom at Lori's house. I questioned my choice in taking such a huge leap and wondered if I had made a mistake, if perhaps I had misunderstood what God was telling me, even though it was so clear to me at the moment it happened. But I couldn't go back now. There was no longer a home to go back to.

4

My drive to find some sort of normal existence would not let me slow down the house-hunting pursuit, and my children were beginning to lose patience with my doggedness. "It took us four years to find our house. Maybe you should move into an apartment while you look for what you want," said Jeff.

"Get rid of your furniture and move in with us," Lori's husband said—on numerous occasions.

"I appreciate your offer, Gary. I really do. But I lost my husband, my home, my friends, everything that identified me as a person. I'd like to have my own space and my belongings from storage so I can enjoy what little I have left of my life."

"You can have your own room and we'll move your stuff in here," he persisted.

"There is no way my belongings will fit in one room. My computer desk, books, and writing materials alone need half that much space," I countered, with mounting exasperation.

Gary didn't understand. None of them did. I was still active and healthy; I wanted to maintain a life of my own for as long as I could. It was sweet of Lori and her family to let me stay in their home. I truly appreciated their kindness and generosity. I also liked having time to enjoy talks with my daughter or play board games with the grandchildren. However, after the sedate life of retirement, it was difficult to get used to the constant activity and noise of a busy, young family again. Living with them on a permanent basis would be a huge adjustment on top of what I had already made. My children were still young enough to see life as an endless road ahead. I had endless life ahead of me, too—in Eternity. At my age, I was a lot closer to Heaven's door than they; maybe that's why we couldn't see things the same way. At any rate none of my children's suggestions was an option for me. Moving into an apartment would eat away at the funds I had for a down payment on a home. Furthermore, most apartment rentals ran as high as, or higher than, a house payment would be. Many evenings, I closed myself in the borrowed bedroom and sent earnest prayers heaven bound. Wait, let me correct myself. The truth is, I *begged* God to speak to me, to send some miracle that would end this madness. My words were sometimes demanding, sometimes pleading but mostly meant the same thing: *Lord, I know you wanted me to make this move and that you must have a house waiting for me here. Why can't I find it? Please, please help me."*

I began to think that although God led me here, maybe He expected me to do my part by finding a house without his help. I eased up on my wish list and was willing not to expect everything I wanted in a home. The next time we went out house-hunting, Melba took me to a house in Mansfield. I really liked the floor plan. The master bedroom had a walk-in closet—something I'd always dreamed about; there was a guest room where my grandkids could come for sleep-overs; another bedroom could serve as my office for doing all my writing and research; and a formal dining room where I could have family dinners now that I was close to family again. However, there were two problems. One was location. The house was near a freeway that was three stories high with roads leading off in all directions. I was nervous about tackling it every time I went to see my children, who wouldn't be as close as I hoped they would be. The second problem was color. The entire house was done in pastel pink and a pale, baby-blue. The bricks on the outside of the house were light pink and all the carpeting was the pale blue color. The kitchen counters were the same shade of blue, and white lace curtains were on the windows. It looked more like a doll house than a place where grownups lived. Melba told me that a little old lady had lived here and recently passed away. The house was left to her children and they all had to agree on the sale. I thought about the cost of replacing the carpeting and counter tops, but I was desperate to be in my own place again so I made an offer on the house and wrote out a check to show my interest.

The next day we took Lori to see the house. She was not enthusiastic about it for the same reasons I felt dubious about whether I was doing the right thing. Later at her house, one of her lady friends was talking with us about my house-hunting woes.

"Why don't you get away from the Dallas area," she said. "And check out some of the little towns south of here, like Waxahachie."

My reaction to that name felt like a light bulb had just turned on in my brain. It was the third time it had been fed to me. Right after Tom died, my writer friend from Flower Mound, Texas, suggested that I move closer to her so we could spend more time together. "There's a little town up this way called Waxahachie. It's a charming place and I think you'd love it there." I didn't follow through on her suggestion because I did not plan on moving out of the San Antonio house.

One year later, when I made my decision to move, the minister in my church mentioned that his grandmother lived in Waxahachie and told me to check it out because it was a nice little town. I could hardly pronounce the name, let alone know what they were talking about. I merely brushed off their suggestions because my goal was to find a home close to my children.

Now the name had been delivered to me for the third time, and I was convinced that God had once again spoken to me through the voice of others. With a map on the front seat of my pickup I headed out to find this place.

Heading south on IH-35, the reverse direction I had traveled to get here, I came to the exit ramp for Waxahachie. And it was just thirty miles from Dallas. Driving through its streets, I fell in love with the town. Small, like the coal-mining town in Pennsylvania where I grew up, it seemed to be welcoming me with open arms. I stopped in a restaurant to have lunch, lingered around town for several hours, and I felt at peace here in a way I hadn't felt for a very long time. As soon as I got back to Lori's house I called Melba and asked her to check into listings for Waxahachie. She found several on the internet and we drove down to see them the next day. But the story was the same. I would have loved to live in one of the beautiful old Victorian homes that the town was noted for, but they cost way beyond what I could afford. All the other houses we looked at needed extensive repairs.

"If you don't mind being away from the downtown area, I know where they're building new homes on the north edge of Waxahachie," Melba said.

"I can't afford a new house with what they cost," I told her. I wondered if she'd had a memory lapse. Hadn't we already established my wobbly financial situation and the high cost of housing?

"We have to pass there on the way back to Lori's house, let's just look," she insisted.

Reluctantly, I agreed.

Highland Village Estates turned out to be an ideal area. Just at the north edge of Waxahachie's city limits, all the businesses and entertainment were just a few minutes drive away, yet it was surrounded by serene farmland. I'd have the best of both worlds here. The development was still under construction, and all the houses were brick—they wouldn't need repairs for a long time. The first one we looked at was almost what I wanted but it had no formal dining room, something I really hoped for so I could have family dinners again. But the salesman made an offer that made me consider it. The government currently had a program with special financing rates and he thought I could qualify. He was going to check on my eligibility and get back to me when he had the information. After we left him, Melba suggested that we go to the next street over, which was in the same development but belonged to a different builder.

"No," I said. "I feel bad that you've spent so much time driving me all over the place, and we've looked at so many houses they're getting jumbled in my brain. I can't remember anymore which ones had what details. I think I can manage with this one if I can get the special financing."

"It won't hurt to look. We're right here. And I want you to be happy," she said.

At this point I didn't really care to look at any more houses, but she was trying so hard to please me that I didn't want to be rude. "Okay, one more stop, then we'll quit for the day."

When I told their salesman what I was looking for, he said, "I have only one house in the size you want. Would you like to see it?"

I said yes.

When we walked through the front door I was hit by such a warm, happy feeling I almost cried. Even before I saw all the rooms, I knew this was the one. It was an identical floor-plan as the one I had seen in Mansfield but this one was done in soft neutral colors. The salesman had only one house in the size I hoped to find and it had everything I wished for. Only *one* house and I knew it was mine. I felt it with such certainty that I could only accept that God had sent another message to me. That became even clearer when Melba's cell phone rang as we were walking through the rooms checking out the amenities. It was the salesman from the place we just left. He was calling to say that I didn't qualify for the government's special financing plan so I couldn't get that house. It didn't matter; I was standing in the one I wanted.

God speaks through heart whispers.

"Melba, can I get out of the offer I made on the Mansfield house?

She smiled at me, "I knew you weren't going to be happy in that house so I never turned in your offer. I'll give your check back to you when we get to my office."

How awesome she was to care enough to keep me from making a mistake. I had certainly done right when I listened to my friend who led me to Melba.

In spite of my assuredness that this was the house for me, it had a six-figure price tag. People from my generation weren't accustomed to paying so much for a home unless they were thought of as extremely wealthy. When Tom and I bought the house in San Antonio in 1975 we paid less than half the amount they were asking for this house. In spite of all the additions and updates we made to that house, the profit I made upon selling it was far below the cost of the one I was looking at. Numbers rolled around in my brain as I gave this some thought. Maybe if I put down the whole amount that I got for the house in San Antonio…and budgeted very carefully…and didn't have any big financial emergencies….

The salesman called their financial officer so I could talk it over with him. The person who arrived looked younger than my children. The first thought in my head was that a youngster like him would never understand my situation and limited budget. He sat down across from me and glanced over my application before looking me in the eye.

"Why are you putting down all this money?" he asked. "This is your money. You need it to live on."

His dark eyes held mine, and the tenderness in them made me feel like I was the youngster and he was promising to take care of me. I'm sure both surprise and relief were wrestling with my facial muscles when I answered him. "I don't think I can afford the payments if I don't."

"Let me worry about that. I know a bank that will go below market rates."

He crunched some numbers on his laptop and came up with a much smaller amount to put down and monthly payments five dollars less than what I told him I could comfortably afford on my widow's benefit and social security checks. I couldn't believe it! Nearly all the houses I had looked at were in the same price range but the financing made the payments too high for me. I could manage this one with no sweat, thanks to a finance officer (another of God's angels?) who did his best to work with my situation.

On June twenty-ninth, I signed the final papers on my new home. Exactly two months earlier, on April twenty-ninth, I had signed final papers on the house I sold in San Antonio. My street address there was 6126; my street address in Waxahachie is 126—the same numbers downsized like my house. Perhaps the quirky numbers were God's humorous way of telling me that I was right about this being the house He had picked out for me and that the journey He invited me on in San Antonio would continue in my new location.

When you think about it, the way I found this place was kind of quirky, too. My writer friend suggested that I move closer to her. Yet she told me to go to Waxahachie, a town fifty miles away from where she lived.

My minister told me to check out Waxahachie where his grandmother lived because he thought I'd be happy there. Later, on a trip to San Antonio, I told him about my house and asked where in Waxahachie his grandmother lived so I could meet her. He said that she actually lived in the nearby town of Ennis. But he had definitely told me to go to Waxahachie.

Finally, Lori's friend told me to go to Waxahachie.

It's clear to me that this is where God wanted me to be. I don't know why he chose Waxahachie, but I guess that will be revealed to me when the time is right with Him.

5

Wanting to know how far the new house was from my children, I clocked the distance to each of their homes. By traveling north on IH-35 then turning east on Highway 20, I could be at Lori's house in forty minutes. If I turned west on 20 instead of east, I'd be at Jeff's home in thirty minutes. I was almost at the halfway point between them. We could visit each other easily and I'd be able to spend lots of time with my grandchildren but I wasn't so close that I'd be babysitting all the time. I love my grandchildren dearly but I was ready to step out of the care-giving mode. This was my time for rest and pursuing neglected dreams. When I asked Melba to find me a home halfway between Lori and my sons, we made the mistake of looking only in towns along the Highway 20 corridor, the road that connects the two cities where they live. God, who knows intimately all the angles and miles of his creation, made His measurements from my needs and desires and moved me to a point south of the Highway 20/ IH-35 intersection, yet still halfway between my children. His wisdom, love, and attention to detail cannot be matched by human minds.

Now that I had a defined goal, I took some of my things to the new house every day. I enjoyed finding places to put them, but I was bursting with eagerness to have the furniture moved in and be settled in my own space. On a Saturday morning, with schedules coordinated and the moving van rented, everyone in Lori's household was up early and roaring to go. As my goods from storage were brought into the new house, the rooms bulged with furniture and boxes. I was never so happy to see my familiar possessions. Lori and Jeff's wife honed in on the cartons marked "kitchen supplies" and got busy putting the kitchen in order while I flitted about showing the men where to place the furniture. All extra stuff was assigned to the garage for what would eventually become a super yard sale. When the U-Haul truck was finally empty, I gathered my family around the dining room table for dinner. After a journey that at times had left me feeling like an uncertain wanderer, I was once again connected to my life. I was home. That night I slept like a baby…in my own bed.

Over the next few weeks, my spirits soared as I put my house in order. To put it more bluntly, I went a little crazy. I was like Picasso with a giant, blank canvas and colors galore. I had no one to please now but myself so I put all my favorite things into play, and I bought some floral fabric to re-cover my favorite recliner and make matching window valances. When I finally had everything like I wanted it, I stepped back and inspected my new domain. Wow! I hadn't realized what an impact the bright, cheerful colors, like red accents in the kitchen, made. My surroundings felt like a celebration after the hard times.

Being in a new place was a fun time. I enjoyed exploring my new surroundings, and learning my way around town. Occasionally I had to drive out of town to accomplish some business, and I was a little nervous about driving on unfamiliar highways to unknown places in the speeding traffic. But the more I tackled, the easier it became. Funny, isn't it, how you lose your fear of getting lost or turning the wrong way down a one-way street once you remember that you can read road signs and drive as well as anyone else—and better than many.

The nearby Chamber of Commerce was a valuable resource, a place I would suggest checking out to anyone moving into a new community. The ladies who worked in the office were friendly and eager to offer help. They were quite knowledgeable on businesses in town, upcoming events and schedules of trade shows, community plays, festivals and so much more. I had found their office on my first visit here. They had given me a Waxahachie road map that day with all the important and useful local sites marked. I used it almost daily. Through their literature I learned that Waxahachie's unique name was derived from the Indian word meaning *cow* or *buffalo*. The famed Shawnee and Chisholm Trails, which had been major cattle trails to the north, ran through the center of Waxahachie, thus giving inspiration for the Indian name.

It was also through the Chamber's brochures that I found out about the Market Days that took place on Saturday mornings around the town square. One Saturday I ventured down to check it out. What an awesome day that turned out to be. The downtown area is a charming place where life is so simple and slowed down that I felt like I had stepped into an old western film. People mulled about the streets not worrying about traffic because drivers moved slowly, giving pedestrians the right of way. Parking was no problem because a whole block just north of the square had been turned into a fenced-in city parking lot for downtown shoppers and community events—and there was no cost to use it. Right across the street from the parking lot was the police station, something I appreciated after leaving the big city and its crime. There was no chance anybody would bother vehicles here.

A huge granite and sandstone courthouse, constructed in 1894, is the crowning glory of the downtown square. Nine stories high, including its impressive bell tower that features a four-faced clock, it towers over the Downtown area. Most early Texas towns were paved with brick streets, and a large portion of Waxahachie's original brick is still part of the intersection at the corner of the courthouse. Before the brick streets, the square had been paved with wood-blocks to quiet the noise of horses' hooves and wagon wheels. Legend claims that Harry Hurley, a stone-carver, was hired to beautify the courthouse. While doing the job, he fell in love with a lady named Mabel Frame. He was so smitten that he carved her lovely face into the arches of the building exterior. Sadly, the love affair did not work out. Harry was so broken-hearted that the remaining faces he carved were sad, angry, evil faces. Many tourists still come to Waxahachie to see the faces of the famous legend on the courthouse.

Amazingly preserved vintage brick buildings edge all four sides of the square. Small shops occupy the lower floors, and storage space or offices are upstairs. Pleasant store owners readily speak to everyone who comes through their door, including me, and I soon knew several of them by first names. Some of the sidewalks were above street level and steps from years gone by led up to them. I had to be careful where I walked because of crumbling cement in some of the steps, not always in a hurry like I shopped in the bustling malls of San Antonio. It was plain to me that Waxahachie had purposely kept as close to its original charm and history as possible, thanks to its dedicated Historical Society. The best way I can describe the scene around the courthouse square is that time had stopped here and the modern world had not filtered in.

Since today was Market Day, the streets around the court house were blocked off to vehicle traffic so farmers and craftsmen could set up their wares for sale. Some were in white tents; others displayed their items on picnic tables or trailers attached to the back of their pickups. It was a sunny day and people lazily ambled through the streets, visiting as well as buying. Most of them, it seemed, knew one another. I, too, walked about at a lazy pace, inspecting the fresh produce and plants, and delighting in the privilege of choosing food that went from the farm directly to my hands. At lunch time I stopped at a hot dog wagon and bought a wiener and soft drink. Finding a shady spot on the low wall around the courthouse lawn, I sat on it to eat. Farmers in overalls and old men and women stopped to talk or sat beside me making comments about the weather and everyday life as though we were friends. I suspected that for the oldsters this trek to Market Days was the highlight of their week. When I had finished my hot dog and drink, I sauntered back across the square toward my pickup. Along the way, I stopped to admire and inhale the fragrance of some hand made soaps being sold by two women. With small-town ease, they immediately struck up a conversation. "Are you from Waxahachie?" one asked.

"I just recently moved here from San Antonio," I said.

"What brought you here?" asked the other.

Hearing the story of how I came here, they were flabbergasted. "Weren't you afraid to come to a place you don't know anything about?" the first inquired.

"And where you don't know anybody?" the second quickly chimed in.

"Not really" I answered. "God is here and I know Him. I feel like He brought me here for some reason." Wide smiles curved across their faces, and they shook their heads in approval. I was in the Bible belt. So unlike the city I had come from, folks here talked about their faith and God as comfortably as they discussed what they were having for dinner.

"You are really brave to make such a move at your age."

"And start a whole new life in a strange place."

I appreciated their support but my heart was already well-grounded in the assurance that I was doing what God wanted me to do. However, I did wonder why God had brought me to this particular town. Not that I minded; I loved it here. I was just curious; why Waxahachie? Was there something here that God wanted me to do, or something that would have an effect on my life? I assumed that would eventually be revealed to me—in God's time.

Instead of going back home along the main drag leading from my house to downtown, I decided to slip out to the edge of the city and take the highway. Without the traffic lights I could be home in mere minutes. Leaving the courthouse square, I turned left on Main Street and found myself in what is known as the West End. Being here was like falling through a time warp and landing in the Victorian Era. Ages-old shade trees with huge trunks and thick, leafy heads bordered both sides of the street. Beyond the trees, massive, ornate Victorian homes with turrets and gingerbread trim reigned in lush green yards with colorful flowerbeds. Although they had been built more than 100 years ago, they looked as new as if the paint was just drying on them. Obviously, great wealth had been spent on these houses, money that had come from the booming cattle business and productive cotton fields of yesteryear, both commodities still evident in the outskirts of Waxahachie. Speed limit signs seemed unnecessary on

Main Street because traffic automatically slowed while passengers momentarily lost themselves in what remains of a bygone era. I, too, was caught up in the ambiance. Wicker chairs with fluffy cushions on the broad wrap-around porches brought forth images of residents relaxing there with cold lemonade in the sweltering afternoons, a cup of evening tea in the chill of autumn. I could almost hear the friendly ghosts of those residents calling to neighbors on other porches while children darted through yards catching fireflies in Mason jars with holes poked in the lids. After the houses, I passed a park, a small hospital, and a golf course before coming to a wooded area that possessed both sides of the street. The thick foliage seemed like a natural barricade that protected the beauty and calm of downtown Waxahachie from the noise and activity of the highway up ahead.

Entering the ramp to IH-35 I headed home, leaving behind peace and tranquility to return to the madness of speeding traffic, exhaust fumes, and the hum of semi-truck tires on hot pavement.

6

After this morning's outing, I was sure of one thing: my love affair for Waxahachie had grown larger. Free space in my garage, however, was growing smaller. As I maneuvered around the disorder to get inside the house, I figured it was time I started using this space for parking my pickup, not wasting the precious amenity as storage for my extra furniture. By now, I'd settled in enough to know what I needed and what I had to get rid of so I scheduled a garage sale. I spent several days marking prices and arranging tables and bulky items so foot traffic could move through the garage easily. Call me smug; I thought I was on top of things. But I was in no way ready for what greeted me early on the morning of my sale. You'd have thought my front yard was Macy's and it was the week before Christmas. Cars were parked at the curb waiting for me long before I opened the garage door. Their occupants were angry that I didn't start the sale before 8 AM. People picked through stuff like they were mining for gold. Some got into arguments over the same item. Others roamed around, poking through roped-off areas of items not for sale, and then tried to bribe me into selling them. I soon realized my customers were expert garage-sale-hunters, and I was uncertain whether it was my household goods or me that was their prey. And boy, could people haggle over prices! I knew I couldn't get what my belongings were worth so I was willing to consider reasonable offers, but I quickly learned that *reasonable* is not a garage-sale word.

Surprisingly, I was caught off-guard by the sadness I experienced watching my treasured pieces, some in almost new condition, leave the driveway. Only then did I realize that I was still having trouble letting go of the life I knew for the one I had now. Grief is a strange thing. You think you've dealt with it, conquered it, and moved on. You're certain after several bouts that you have. But like unrelenting ocean waves pounding the sandy shores, it keeps coming back at the most unexpected times. I was beginning to understand grief would always be a part of me and would require different ways to be dealt with each time it appeared. I hoped that one day it would gently fall asleep and never wake again. By the day's end I felt like I'd been squeezed through a wringer. My pocketbook was a little fuller but my brain was in chaos. My body had reached its capacity to absorb any more of the heat and sweat that comes with being stuck in the garage for the whole of a hot summer day. No more garage sales for me.

Getting rid of the excess items was a big accomplishment. I was glad it was behind me, but as a home owner, there would always be something new to add to my "to-do" list. The back patio was so tiny it barely accommodated a lawn chair. It needed enlarging if I was going to invite the family over for barbecues or if I just wanted to sprawl out on my lounge chair and read. A cover would also be nice to cut down on the intense Texas heat that flooded the patio and poured into the living room picture window with the setting sun. That quickly expanding list, however, would have to wait. I'd been working hard for weeks, and I was ready to think about something less strenuous—something I really missed: a church home. That was as important to me as finding a place to live. I was well aware that I had come from a military environment in a huge city to a place that was an extreme opposite. Could I find a church here that offered the bonding and good friends, the peace and joy, I had experienced in the church I left behind or would I have to make more sacrifices?

I had not been raised in a religious family. My parents did not attend church and we didn't read the Bible in our house or say grace before meals, but mother did send my sisters and me to Sunday school every week. I had wonderful teachers at the centuries-old, one-room wooden chapel in the hometown of my youth, and the seeds they planted stayed with me as I grew older, especially after I went out on my own. Further reinforcement came from an aunt and uncle who were childless and with whom I spent weekends and summer vacations. I attended their church with them and became involved in its youth activities. I learned about God but I didn't develop a deep personal relationship with Him until years later. When I married an Air Force Sergeant, I joined Protestant Women of the Chapel (PWOC), a world-wide military group. Through these women, I learned the power of prayer, experienced spiritual retreats, and began to understand how a faithful connection to God could change one's life. It didn't come overnight. It grew with years of being exposed to loyal, dedicated Christian friends who supported me as I raised my children, who were there when my mother—and later my husband—died, friends who saw me through many crises and celebrated all my joys as if they were their own. Eventually, I served as president of our local PWOC for one year.

When Tom retired from the Air Force and we settled into a civilian community in San Antonio, I joined Chapel Hill United Methodist Church. Located just outside the back gate of Lackland Air Force Base, its congregation consisted of many of my military friends. For nearly thirty years Chapel Hill, with its close, supporting members, had been my comforting haven. Unfortunately my husband would not join me. Tom believed there was a God but he had very negative feelings about "organized religion," as he called it. In no way did he want to attend church or associate with people who did. I felt like I led two different lives, one at church or in the company of Christian friends, the other at home with my husband. I wanted Tom and me to have the same connection I saw in other couples worshipping together; I wanted to have him sitting at my side and understand the feelings I had about my faith. Throughout our marriage, I had begged God for understanding: *Dear Lord, after so many repeated prayers over the years, why won't you help my husband become a Christian to share the wonder of faith with me?* Unfortunately it didn't happen. Sometimes God's answer is silence. I figured that I'd have to wait until I got to Heaven for my answer to this Question.

Tom's mother, too, prayed faithfully that her son would have a relationship with God. Having died one week before Tom's death, she didn't see that happen. However, thanks to caring, daily visits and prayers from Charles Posey while Tom was on hospice care, he finally made peace with God on his death bed. Our Chaplain friend accomplished what nobody else could. It was a beautiful moment and the change in Tom was immediately obvious to our family when we approached his bed. The pain frown had disappeared from his forehead, his face muscles relaxed, and fear was no longer present in his eyes. He was as peaceful as a sleeping newborn baby. I was thrilled for Tom but his transformation came too late for me to share this new life with him. Tom died shortly after his conversion.

When I moved to Waxahachie, I knew it would be tough to replace the kind of camaraderie I had in the church in San Antonio. Flipping through the Waxahachie phone book, I found two listings for United Methodist churches and checked out both of them during worship services on different Sundays. One was huge and obviously had a wealthy congregation, too many people to notice a visitor in the crowd. It felt formal and regimented, not the kind of worship where I'd feel comfortable. The other church was small and quaint but had lots of empty pews that caused me concern about why it had such a small following.

On my second visit to the little church, the choir director was leading the singing of Emmaus praise songs as I walked in the door, a warm-up that preceded the morning service. I had been on an Emmaus Walk, a deeply-moving weekend retreat in the United Methodist Church and many others. Music is a joyful part of worship to me, but when I don't know the melody, I hesitate to join in the singing. This morning's Emmaus songs were familiar; I could sing along. Scanning the church bulletin, I saw that the choir director's name was Dee Taylor, the same name spelled the same way as a lady in my San Antonio church. The Dee Taylor back there was a cheerful person who loved working with the youth; she was also an acquaintance of Tommy so when I heard that name again I felt a connection. Actually, it was more than that; I had a strong feeling that God was using this similarity to say, "You can have friends here like the friends you had in your last church." I took that to understand that this is where He wanted me to worship.

God even uses little things like a name to send messages.

I know readers will argue that the same name of both women was merely coincidence. But I was following blindly on this journey with God and I needed constant signs, or directions, to know I was doing what He expected of me. You could say I am a lot like Gideon in the Bible. When God asked him to lead his army into Midian and take over the land for Israel, Gideon asked God for a sign that it was really God talking to him. God gave him a sign. Then Gideon asked for another, saying, *"I will place a wool fleece on the threshing floor. If there is dew only on the fleece, and all the ground is dry, then I will know that you will save Israel by my hand, as you have said." And that is what happened.*

The next morning Gideon asked God for still another sign. *"Do not be angry with me. Let me make just one more request. Allow me one more test with the fleece. This time make the fleece dry and the ground covered with dew." That night God did so. (Judges 6: 37-40)*

I'm not quite as needy as Gideon was but I do need to hear God's voice within me or at least see something that shows me He is still leading me. The same-name incident was that sign and it helped me understand that God wanted me to choose this church in which to worship. I hoped that eventually I would learn why.

When the service ended that morning and I was leaving, a friendly lady approached me and introduced herself as Joyce McNeely. "Would you like to come to my Sunday school class?" she asked. "They're all seniors, like you and I; we'd love to have you join us."

I did join them the following Sunday, and I liked the group enough to become a regular member. It's a very close knit group, as caring and supportive of each other as if we were one big family. Nearly all of the members have lived in this area for most of their lives so they know each other and their families well, and they accepted me as warmly as if I had grown up with them. The other classes refer to us as "The Old People's class." Most of us have bifocals, hearing aids, dentures, grey hair, and have celebrated seventy or eighty plus birthdays. Our oldest member is ninety-five. We love God, life, and celebrating our togetherness with two big outings each year. This summer, for instance, we went to the Texas Theater where we joked with the actors and laughed out loud over the memories revived by the 50's style play. After the show, we gathered at Braum's and ate ice-cream loaded with cholesterol while we talked across the aisles like noisy teenagers after a Friday night game. Around Christmas we'll be somewhere around town whoopin' it up again for our second annual gathering of the year.

Upon finding this church home in addition to all the other good things that had been happening for me, I felt sure I was in the right place. But just in case I was still in doubt, God kept sending me messages, like the evening I attended a United Methodist Women's meeting at the church. A lady named Cheryl asked what brought me to

Waxahachie (Everyone, it seemed, wanted to know that). After hearing my story she said, "God kept you at your daughter's house so long because the house He had for you wasn't ready yet. You had to wait until it was finished being built."

I hadn't thought about it until she said the words. She was right. This house in Waxahachie that was so perfect for me had just been completed when Melba and I found it. In fact, the builder's sawhorse was still sitting across the driveway to keep people from going inside. Cheryl's words reminded me how discouraged I had become while at Lori's and how I had emotionally pleaded with God to help me find a place to live. And all that time God *was* preparing a house for me. But He was using human hands that could only work within human limits and time. Cheryl's words not only helped me to see this but on giving them more thought I realized I was being taught a lesson. That lesson was that I needed to have more patience and to trust God more completely. There was no reason to get fearful or discouraged. He was walking beside me on this journey, and He was leading. My job was to follow and obey.

God speaks through angels.

Though I didn't know it at the time, the biggest influence this church would have on my life came from a young woman named Dana. She was young enough to be my daughter, but she invited me to join her Christian book-study group. Dee Taylor, the choir director, was also a member of the group. I was a little hesitant because I didn't know how a grandma like me would fit in with the younger women. What could I lose? If it didn't work out, I could always quit; it wasn't a contract deal.

7

Women need girlfriends. It's our nature. When we're troubled and need someone to talk to, we know we can trust them and they won't judge us. When we're happy, we know they will drop everything to celebrate with us. Girlfriends make the good times better, and the bad times easier because you share them with each other. It didn't take long to realize that the six women in our book club would become the best of girlfriends. Though we were so diverse in personalities and ages, the intimate environment and the relationships we quickly formed glued our small group together. Our meetings were held at Dee's house. Dee was in an accident at the age of nineteen and broke her back, leaving her lower body paralyzed. She has been confined to a wheelchair ever since. Her home is wheelchair friendly. Ours aren't, so hers was the natural place to meet. The gifts and weaknesses each of us brought to this union made it function like clock-work.

Dee was our self-proclaimed mediator who helped explain differing opinions so emotions would stay calm. She has a remarkable attitude about her limitations and says getting to know her and how she copes helps people see they can do anything they set their minds to. Dee has a faith that could conquer anything. She works as a special education teacher for behavioral students and is suited to the job like a glove to fingers. No matter how dysfunctional her students are, they all come to love Dee, which most likely results from her genuine concern for each of them. Nobody can be in her presence for more than a few minutes without getting caught up in her spontaneous laughter. Her attitude teaches the rest of us much about life. When asked her opinion of our group, Dee said, "I get love, understanding, guidance, help, hope, differing points of view, laughter and a hard time. I also get to have the closeness of sisters that I don't have with my biological sisters."

Dana and Dee, both in their forties, are best friends, and they often get distracted with their goofing around or irritating one another at our cluster. That's okay; our meetings are for being ourselves. Dana is a paraprofessional who oversees In-School-Suspension at a Jr. High School. Her students are the ones who make poor choices and get caught making them. She is the right person for the job. A strong disciplinarian, she doesn't get distracted from her purpose in being there or in the important life lessons these students need to learn. Dana brings a whole new vocabulary to our group. One of the most honest people I've met, she has no problem telling you exactly what she thinks—without hurting your feelings. Sometimes, her words raise our eyebrows; other times they send us into hysterical laughter. For example, she once brought a picture of herself dressed in a full-skirted, gold taffeta dress she wore to a family wedding. Her comment was, "I looked like a large, golden roast!" Because of Dana, we named our group *The Ditto Daughters*. Often during a discussion she gives her opinion with a mere "Ditto." It became such a novelty that we all started using it. Ditto had to be part of our name. Dana says of our group, "It's the place to come for great advice, friends who listen, and help through tough times."

Janie, beautiful and full of grace, is our pastor's wife. She has shared with us the struggles put upon her by people who have stereotypical ideas of how clergy wives should dress and act, and the hurt she has suffered because of their interpretations. I had not realized that this apparently common trait went on among parishioners. Janie is just a regular person, a mother and grandma, no different than other women. Her emotions are just below the surface and animatedly break through on both joyous and sad occasions. She is a joy to be around. Her wisdom in relating a Bible passage to whatever personal struggle one of us might be experiencing amazes me. Another gift she brings to the group is her counseling expertise. As a career counselor at a university, she often knows the perfect advice or encouragement for a group member who might need it.

Sherry is a Senior Loan Processor for a mortgage firm, and when called upon, she gives us sage legal advice about money matters and mortgage information. She is the quiet one, the person who always appears to be happy even when she's had a bad day. Her hope is that she has given group members insight into sharing the same problems no matter how our ages differ. "I enjoy the fellowship and different attitudes we each have on the subjects we discuss and feel a real kinship to all the "dittos," she says.

Donna is the youngest of our group, a divorcee and single mom who's had a rough life. She's the kind of person who wants to help anyone in a bad situation, to the point where she forgets to take care of herself and her own needs at times. Donna is passionate about life and learning how to be what God wants her to be. Like Janie, she is quick to connect Bible verses to topics we may be discussing. One of the happiest domestic-help workers I have ever seen Donna not only loves her occupation, she is remarkably good at turning a house into organization and sparkle.

I, being the oldest, offer advice from my sixty plus years of experience. Widely traveled as an Air Force wife, I lived among many cultures; I was a volunteer at a Rape Crisis Center; I was a Registered Nurse for many years; and, as part of the generation that lived during World War II, I remember what it was like not to have all the technology that is present today; we learned to improvise in all we did. I wasn't sure if my experiences were of value to this lively group but one evening Dana said that seeing how I am starting a whole new life in my late years inspires her and makes her feel more confident about her future. I consider that to be the best compliment to get from a girlfriend.

As you can see we are a varied group. We have different personalities, talents, and backgrounds. What binds us together is our desire to know God better. Our meetings are a safe haven for girls' night out, a time for discussion and finding answers, and an opportunity to support one another when life throws us a curve or ills strike. I wish everyone could have a group like this. The books we study are accounts of other Christians' personal experiences. Seeing how others learned to cope with life's struggles and overcome them is helpful in dealing with our own troubles. One or more of our group members always identify with the authors whose books we study. It is hard not to see God's hand in putting together this group of women. We all needed each other for different reasons, and we all loved our Lord. We trusted one another enough to be at ease about bringing up personal problems; we know whatever we say here stays here. None of us has had difficulty being totally honest when we discuss private matters, as well as the reading materials we study. Don't get me wrong. Ours is definitely not a gathering of religious fanatics having private psychobabble conferences; some evenings we are just plain silly. On these nights, we set aside our books and enjoy just goofing off and having a laugh or two. There are no better stress-relievers than chilling out with dear friends.

As a newcomer, the group helped me learn about businesses in my new locale. They gave me the name of a good hairdresser and gynecologist, also an optometrist. They told me how to get to the nearest mall; there were only two small department stores with limited stock in Waxahachie. And when we were going someplace outside of Waxahachie, they always picked me so I wouldn't get lost. I counted on them a lot during my settling in period.

After we'd been meeting for some time, Dee became very mysterious concerning something she had in mind. She didn't reveal it to us until a night when we hadn't planned to meet. We had just finished the book we were studying and needed to figure out a time when all of us could go to the Christian book store to choose another one, so we suspended meetings until that could be accomplished. But Dee contacted each of us and told us to come to her house the next Monday night at our usual time. She wouldn't say why. Throughout the week whenever one of us would bump into someone from the group, the first question asked was, "Do you know what Dee has planned?" Her secret was safe. Nobody knew.

When we arrived, the formal dining room table was aglow with an array of candles. Angel figures randomly placed among them added a special touch. Each place setting included a wine glass filled with grape juice, a fancy hand-made booklet with the words *Monday Night Ditto Daughters* inscribed on the cover, and a costume-jewelry gold ring featuring a rainbow of colored stones. After we were welcomed and seated, we took turns around the table saying what the group studies had meant to us. Then we spent some time reminiscing over highlights of our meetings. At times, the sharing was deeply moving; other times it was downright goofiness that set us off to giggling. Finally, we recited together a pledge that Dee had written in the little booklets:

We the Ditto Daughters pledge to be there for each other, to show God's love to each other by our actions and prayers. We will hold out a helping hand when needed...

Lend a listening ear, book, air pump, car, purse, an occa-
sional hat or top, or our heart... Be brutally honest when
required—and sometimes necessary. Until death or taxes
separate us from each other, we now pledge our troubles,
joys, laughter, and prayers in God's Holy name. Amen.

This handful of women grounded me, and I had come
to rely heavily on their friendship. A short time ago I was
in an unfamiliar town full of strangers. Now I had five
endearing friends who had truly become my sisters and
supporters. I could call upon any of them any time I was
in trouble or just wanted another woman to talk to, and
I knew they'd respond. God outdid himself in providing
friends and a church family that made me feel loved and
gave me a sense of belonging. But although I had these
wonderful new friends, I was still attached to the ones
I left In San Antonio, and apparently they felt the same
way about me. One evening I received a call from Jim and
Shirley, a couple who had been friends of our family for a
long time.

"We're making plans to go on a cruise through the
Panama Canal, and we wondered if you would like to go
with us?" said Shirley.

Jim was on their other phone and the two of them tripped over each other's words as they filled me in on the details of the two-week cruise. Shirley's old college friend was also a widow and interested in going on the cruise. They thought that she and I might share a shipboard cabin which would make the trip more affordable for us. While taking in all their enticing words, I was excited, but hesitant. The cost of a two-week cruise seemed phenomenal to me, and I had just spent a lot of money in a very short time with buying the house and all I needed to complete it inside and out.

"You've been through two rough years" urged Shirley. "The vacation will do you good. The trip is not until next April, months away, so you have a long time to put some money aside."

"But we don't want you to feel pressured," added Jim. "Think about it and let us know." Jim is the world's biggest tease with an underlying worry about hurting people's feelings—or not!

Think about it, I did—all the time. Even, more so when Shirley's college friend, Raye, called from Minnesota and introduced herself. We spent a long time on the phone that evening, and there was no doubt that we'd make compatible traveling partners if I decided to go. Conversation between us came easily, and we discovered we had a lot in common besides our widow status. She, too, had a slew of grandchildren and the accompanying Grammy syndrome. Like me, she liked to power walk. She enjoyed reading; I liked to write books. And we had the connection of both being good friends of Shirley and Jim, though she knew them much longer than I did. During several of our conversations, we tickled the phone lines with laughter over stories we shared about past interactions with them. It only took me a couple days of thinking about it before I made up my mind. I called Shirley and told her to count me in.

During the time we had before our sailing date, the four of us kept the internet busy with e-mails. When we weren't doing that we were on the phone, planning what side trips we would take when the ship visited ports. Since Shirley and her husband reserved a balcony cabin, Raye and I did the same. That way all of us could be close together or at least on the same deck. The way we all agreed with one another made it obvious that we were a winning foursome.

After deciding I was actually going on this cruise, my enthusiasm soared. Seizing the moment, I decided to update my wardrobe for clothing that would be suitable for such an excursion. For one thing, there would be two formal nights, for which I would need a gown or cocktail dress—something I hadn't worn in years. I had a grand girlie-time shopping and found a great red cocktail dress and an ankle-length navy gown with a sequin top for the formal occasions. No out-of-style old lady was I going to be. I also found some cute tops that would mix and match with slacks or skirts. When I wasn't shopping I studied the cruise brochures. The idea of passing through the famous canal and seeing how it worked was enough to blow my mind. I didn't know how I would contain my eagerness through the long wait until our departure date. I was ready to leave now.

Then I received a huge and unexpected bombshell that wiped all thoughts of sailing out of my head. My Sunday school class needed a teacher to replace one that left the church, and they asked if I'd take over. Me, a Sunday school teacher? Not in my wildest dreams! If God was behind this He sure had a sense of humor. It wasn't talking to the class that panicked me, I had given all those presentations and media interviews when my books were published, and I had that acting class under my belt, which gave me more confidence. But being a Sunday school teacher was a whole different ballgame. I didn't feel in any way qualified to teach scripture and life lessons to a group of Christian seniors that were probably more knowledgeable about the topic than I. Though I had a good Sunday school teacher when I was growing up, and attended church faithfully when I became an adult, I had never read the entire Bible or memorized many scripture verses. I seriously did not think I was capable of being a teacher. They reminded me that I would not have to teach every Sunday. Because it is difficult to find someone to do this service, we have four teachers. One teaches on the first Sunday every month (and the fifth when there is one); another teaches on the second Sundays; another on the third; and I would be responsible for the fourth Sunday every month. The class members persisted until they convinced me to at least be a facilitator until they found a teacher. What this meant, they explained, was someone to lead the group while everyone gave their input on the lesson of the day. To that I agreed.

Teaching didn't come easy. And planning the lessons was time-consuming even though I had a very good teacher's guide. Every week, I prayed for God to use my voice to relay His message. He always came through. I was often able to use one of my personal experiences as an example that tied in with the day's lesson, and class members told me it helped them understand better. The job has remained mine ever since I started. It has been an awesome experience, and the research in preparation for each lesson has helped me understand the Bible and God better. The closer I grow to Him through this experience, the more outgoing and happy I become. John Ruskin, the great Victorian poet and philosopher once quoted, "The highest reward for a person's toil is not what they get for it, but what they become by it."[1] This experience has shown me how true that is. Having had this role bestowed upon me, I ask God once again, *Is this why you brought me to Waxahachie?* But God never answers that question. I guess He doesn't feel like it's necessary to do so. Maybe He brought me here for all these reasons—the full package, as a salesman might say.

8

Whenever I reflect back on my journey with God I realize anew the depth of His goodness, the uncertainties that had been resolved, the helpers who had been put in my path, and the little miracles that got me through. I felt that it was time for me to pass on the goodness that I had been given, something bigger than teaching the Sunday school class. While I was thinking about what I might do, the minister sent out a call for members to find ways they could become more involved in doing the tasks necessary for running a church. She passed around a paper listing openings on different committees or other areas needing help. I am not a committee person; I work better on my own so I thought about what I might do. Immediately my writing came to mind. We needed a communicator to get notices put in the local newspaper or on the radio, so I offered to write up those and send them in. Then I took it a step further. I keep a journal and many of my articles have a God connection because they are about stressful or joyous times in the life of me and my family. I thought I'd like to use these or do similar writings as a devotional column for the church's monthly newsletter. That was accepted with eagerness. Through the years I have continued to do the columns, and I receive so much feedback that it inspires me to keep at it and do my best. I now have a large collection of them in my portfolio and hope to share them with others one day by putting them in a book collection.

With my teaching and writing tasks, I felt like I was sharing the work load necessary to keep a church going. But I wanted to do more for God by getting involved in some type of community service where I could serve others. I scanned the local newspaper hoping to find something that matched my interests and abilities. One very short notice in small print ran often and always caught my attention. The Gingerbread House, which is Ellis County's Children's Advocacy Center, was looking for volunteers, and they offered training for the position. I kept looking at other possibilities but my eyes were always drawn back to that little bitty ad. There obviously was a need, and I was qualified for the position. I love children, and with my big family I had lots of experience with little ones. I had also worked as a volunteer for three years in a rape crisis center in San Antonio where some of the victims I worked with were sexually abused children. And, as a nurse I often worked on the children's ward. I thought the position at the Gingerbread House might be just what I was looking for. However, when I mentioned it to my Ditto Daughters group they warned me that dealing with abused children could be difficult, haunting me with their sad faces and the ugly events in their lives.

"Why don't you try going to the local grade schools?" suggested Dee. "They're always looking for grandma types to read to the kids or help them with their homework."

"I don't know," I answered, mulling it over in my head. For some reason volunteering in the elementary school didn't excite me. Maybe it was the mother or grandma in me that wanted to be involved with an organization whose goal was to stop the abuse of children. Or maybe it was the retired nurse that was drawn more to the caregiver situation than the classroom. At any rate, I answered the ad for the Gingerbread House and when the next training session was scheduled, I attended. The center, I learned, is a safe place where a multi-disciplinary team, including Law Enforcement Agencies, the District Attorney's Office, Child Protective Services, and the County Juvenile Services can investigate child abuse cases without subjecting the young victims to repeated interviews and re-victimization. Children of suspected sexual or violent physical abuse are brought to the center where they are interviewed by "Miss Teresa," a professional Forensic Interviewer, in a private, child-oriented room. She is a master at easing the children into comfortable conversation, questioning them while they draw pictures together with colored markers (The drawings are easy ways the children can refer to private parts without having to experience the discomfort of explaining verbally what happened to them). During this interaction the interview is being videotaped and transmitted to an adjoining room where the multi-disciplinary team observes and evaluates the information the child gives. This is how they determine if they have enough evidence to bring charges against the abuser, thus ending the abuse.

My job would be as a "family greeter." Hours were uncertain; I'd be on call five days a week in case a child was brought in. But as a volunteer, I wouldn't have to go if I got called when I already had some appointment or other plans for that day. I would also be responsible for providing the paperwork to the adult who brought the child or children in and help them if they didn't understand something on the forms. I'd offer them coffee or a bottle of water. Most importantly, as the first person to approach the children, I'd help put them at ease and entertain them while they waited to be interviewed. Sometimes, I'd have to help with fund raisers or office work and help keep the playroom straightened up. It seemed pretty simple, and since I had no one to answer to at home, my time was as flexible as their schedule.

On my first case, I was nervous, uncertain whether establishing rapport with children, who were already traumatized, would be difficult. But after a few times, I was totally at ease. Most of the little ones liked to build blocks so I get down on the floor and join them, like I do with my grandkids. Sometimes we watch videos or read story books. Older children usually just want to watch a movie or talk about school or sports; maybe they don't talk at all—it is always harder for the older victims to talk about what happened. When it's time for the victims to be interviewed, I visit with the adults who brought them in. They aren't allowed to go back in the interview room with the children so they're usually apprehensive while waiting for them to return. It helps to distract them with conversation or just be a willing listener. The adults always need to talk about their feelings—often it's about the guilt they feel for not knowing the abuse was happening—and my past experience as a psychiatric nurse along with a big helping of compassion is all I need to help them.

Not all children that come through the center are abused; some turn out to be false alarms. Sometimes, the ones who are abused are too traumatized to open up and talk about it to Miss Teresa. Without adequate information the case can't go any further. They're the heart-breaking ones. But considering the phenomenal amount of kids seen at the center, the success rate of arrests is very high, and the counseling references are a blessing to the victims and their families. I rely on the hope that I am, too. If I can give these young victims one hour of fun in a safe, threat-free environment then I am where I'm supposed to be. Even though I don't spend a lot of time with each one, I feel good about touching their lives in a positive way. How do I know I've done this? It's when I see the relieved look on the face of parents when I've answered their questions in a satisfactory way or given them information that will give them hope. The little ones make me feel like I'm impacting their lives, too, like the little tot who was leaving after her interview and ran back to throw their arms around my legs in a hug. I'm convinced that God kept pulling me back to that little newspaper ad because He needed me to love and comfort His hurting people.

God speaks through written words.

Still, I feel like what I'm doing is such a small thing so once again, I ask *Is this why you brought me here, God?*

As the days passed I grew more and more certain that moving to this little country town was one of the happiest choices I made. Reveling in my new freedom, I ate what I wanted, when I wanted. I stayed up late or turned in very early. Some days I slept in; others, I rose just after dawn and went walking. I became more outgoing and adventuresome. When I felt like going someplace, I jumped in my pickup and took off without worrying about when I had to get back home. Life was good and, like a kid in a candy shop, I wanted all I could get of it. Fun became an active subject in my days, and when Sharon, a neighbor, sent out notices questioning if anyone would be interested in throwing a block party, I got excited. Our housing area was still under construction and many of the completed homes were not yet occupied. Our street, however, already had eleven families in residence. Sharon thought the block party would be a good way to get acquainted.

Several women met on her lawn and made plans. It was agreed that each family would put their grills in the front driveway where the guys could cook their family's meat. The women were responsible for providing a casserole or other food item to share. I was asked to get in touch with the city manager and see if it would be okay to block off traffic on our street the night of the party. The city was not only in favor of the idea but they offered to send people out to put up barricades on the assigned night.

When the date arrived, the street was full of people and activity. Several families had put wading pools or water slides in their yards for the youngsters. One family provided a bounce house. Someone offered a large canopy to keep the food table covered and there was plenty of it, in a wide variety of choices. The canopy was placed across from my house, since I lived opposite the only lot still remaining empty on this street. With the food crowd gathering in my area, I put extra lawn chairs in the driveway and was thrilled to have people I hadn't seen before come sit with me for a spell. All evening, mouth-watering odors wafted from smoking bar-b-q grills. Somewhere, music was playing. Small groups gathered along the street, talking and laughing. Little ones were running all over the place without worry of watching for cars. The city police stopped by to see how things were going and we invited them to help themselves to the food. It was a wonderful evening, the kind where one would expect Opie and Aunt Bea to come wandering down the road at any moment. The event lasted into darkness when people gradually sauntered, a few at a time, back inside—only because mosquitoes, the Texas heat, and tired youngsters required it.

Sitting alone in my living room I relived the event in my head and felt such joy at having had this experience. It was such a simple thing, people sharing their lives, their time, some food, yet it was so meaningful. Small-town Texas was swallowing me up and I thrived on every new occurrence presented to me. Living here is a huge change from living in a big city where crime and jammed highways are common. At the bottom of my street, there is a creek that meanders through a lush, wooded area; farmland borders the top of the street. While I'm eating breakfast by the bay window in my kitchen, I see amazing sunrises over the treetops across the street. No tall buildings to block the scenery here. William Penn, the founder of Pennsylvania, defined this lifestyle aptly when he stated, "The country life is to be preferred, for there we see the works of God; but in the cities little else but the works of men."[2]

As I marked off the days until my cruise date, I enjoyed quiet times alone in my cozy abode, watching all the chic shows on TV. The remote was mine! My most loved program was "What Not to Wear;" my favorite channel became HGTV (Home and Garden Television). I perused magazines uninterrupted, and had lengthy phone calls with

Traveling Interstate Highway 35 With God

my buddies. But I also wanted to stay active and be connected to others instead of just lazing around and growing old. Fortunately, little nudges and unsuspected offerings kept coming along to fill my social calendar. My sister-in-law mentioned that she had joined Curves, a fitness center for women, and was really enjoying it so I checked to see if there was one in Waxahachie. Not only did I find one but it was just a few blocks from my house. I signed up for a membership. Working on the resistance machines and doing floor exercises made me feel good. I always left there feeling rejuvenated and full of energy. Then a member of my Sunday school class told me she belonged to a seniors' line-dancing group that met at the YMCA. I decided to give that a try. However, the first encounter quickly changed my understanding of the word *seniors*. Before each session, an elderly gentleman put everyone through warm-up exercises that were done while sitting on a chair. One example was to cross one knee over the other, then circle our ankle, first in one direction then the other. Another was to open and close our fingers several times. While still seated, we would put one foot out and tap the floor, then bring it back and repeat it with the other

121

foot, as though doing a dance step sitting down. This was exercise? Perhaps I was being flippant but I didn't want to be that kind of senior, not now that I had an exciting new life. I tried to skip the warm-up session by showing up late, hoping they'd be finished with the exercise when I arrived. They waited for me! To make matters worse, I was having a terrible time learning their routines. The leader's only instruction for me was to learn by watching what they were doing. But the steps were very different from my San Antonio line-dancing class. These women had been working together for a long time; they scooted along in perfect precision. I was so busy trying to figure out what they were doing that I couldn't keep up. I felt like the class klutz. I decided this wasn't for me. That was okay; I found other activities; our Ditto Daughters met on Monday night. I hooked up with an Emmaus Reunion group which met for breakfast on Saturday mornings, and I joined a co-ed Bible study on Saturday evenings. Best of all, I was close enough to Lori, Jeff, and Tommy to visit often. Some days I stayed for a few hours, other times I spent the night. Having five grandchildren in this area was a delight.

In this whirlwind of activity an old friend began to nag me: my writing—more specifically my neglected manuscripts. I had been unable to spend time on them during Tom's illness and the ensuing numbness of his loss. Now that I tried again, my passion for arranging words on paper jumped back to life. I was elated when I saw a writers' group advertised in the newspaper. I joined them, taking care of my Thursday evenings.

I have come a long way in the last two years and landed in a dream existence. Truly, each day is like an ongoing celebration of life. I think I've earned this time. I raised five children, cared for my mother while she had Alzheimer's disease, helped with my grandchild when her parents divorced, nursed my husband at home until the day cancer snuffed out his last breath, and I gave a helping hand to anyone I could along my road of life. I don't feel guilty about using this time now to nourish my soul and become the person God intended me to be. Every woman deserves that. However, I'm not smug enough to expect my life to always be this good. Fate can throw bumps in the road. It's inevitable I'll have a few of those to climb over. And God, being God, can drop a surprise in my lap at any time; I don't' know what might be required of me to meet another challenge. Furthermore, I must admit that in spite of all the goodness and contentment, there's still a tiny place deep within me that pesters my mind during quiet moments: *What was God's reason for bringing me to this place?*

9

When I walked into my Sunday school class on the first Sunday of the New Year, I immediately noticed a newcomer talking to Joyce McNeely's husband. There was no way I could have missed him; he was standing right in the middle of the room beneath the ceiling fan, as if he had been staged there. He was about my age, very handsome, slim, and well dressed. Other class members seemed to know him but I had not seen him here in the six months I'd been coming to this class. Something within me said to pay attention to this man. I didn't have to guess where those words came from. I knew. But this heart whisper caught me so off-guard that I was both surprised and confused. Pay attention to this man? What exactly did that mean? I found my seat and tried to act like it was any other Sunday morning, it didn't work. When the visitor took a seat at the opposite end of the table from where I was sitting, I couldn't stop from stealing glances of him. I'm grateful that nobody could hear the crazy dialog that was going on in my head, as I wondered who this guy was and why he'd shown up so suddenly, or if he had a partner somewhere in the church. Though I couldn't deny my interest in him, I didn't want to get involved with another man. I was living the perfect existence; partners complicated things.

When the class ended, Joyce called me over to meet Weldon Phillips. "He lives right down the street from your house. Since you were a military wife I thought you might be able to help him figure out how to get his medications at the Veteran's Hospital to save on costs."

"I was in the Army a long time ago," Weldon explained when we were alone. "I'm diabetic and also take medication for high blood pressure. My wife always took care of things like this for me, but she died a year ago from lung cancer. Friday will be the one-year anniversary of her death."

"I know how hard that is. It's been a little under two years since my husband died of lung cancer," I said.

"Unfortunately, I don't think I can be of any help with the medications. I always got my prescriptions filled at the Air Force Base pharmacy. I don't know if the regulations are the same for Veterans' Hospitals. Is there one near here?"

"There's one in Lancaster, not far from here, but I guess Joyce doesn't understand that they won't fill my prescriptions unless I use their doctors. I used to go to a doctor there but it was such a hassle that I switched to a civilian doctor some time ago."

I understood what he was talking about. I had used military medical facilities since marrying Tom—a benefit he earned for spending twenty-two years active duty in the Air Force and serving during two wars. Military doctors change duty stations frequently, and replacements take over their patient load. The new doctors aren't familiar with your medical history so it's like starting all over again every few visits.

"I'll probably just stay with my civilian doctor," Weldon added. "I can manage the cost of the medication for now."

My encounter with him had been brief but all that week I couldn't stop thinking about his beautiful blue eyes and shy smile. Part of me kept wishing the next Sunday would hurry and get here, but another part kept fighting the feelings. I wasn't even sure Weldon would be back to our church. But he did live just down the road; surely we'd bump into each other somewhere. Maybe we could meet for a cup of coffee; nothing wrong with two people who live alone sharing some neighborly conversation and a little time with each other.

For the next two weeks, I saw Weldon only at church, and very briefly at that. But on the third Sunday, he came to sit beside me in the worship service following Sunday school. During that glorious hour, I noticed everything about him: the way he sat with one leg stretched out before him, his brown cowboy boots, and his low base voice when we sang hymns. Sitting there beside him felt so right that I didn't want the hour to end. Four days later, I was sitting in front of my TV when the phone rang. The sound of Weldon's voice made me as excited as a school girl with her first crush. You'd think after so many years of living and mingling with people that I'd be able to carry on a simple phone conversation with a neighbor. Nothing was further from the truth. I couldn't think of anything clever or entertaining to say, and when I did speak, I fell all over my words. This was Thursday; he invited me to go out for dinner on Saturday. Of course, I accepted.

"Tomorrow night I'm going to the girls' basketball game at the high school," he said, extending our conversation.

"Do you know someone who plays for them?"

"No, but I like to go to the games. Waxahachie has a good team."

"That sounds interesting," I said, remembering how I enjoyed going to professional basketball games during my youth, before life and motherhood changed my priorities.

"Would you like to go?" he asked.

"If you don't mind, I'd really like that."

"I'll pick you up about six."

You never saw a more nervous person than I was the next evening. I spent way too much time on make-up and hair-combing, and wondered what I'd gotten myself into. I was in no way ready for the dating scene. *It isn't really a date*, I reminded myself. *Just two lonely people getting together for some relaxation and companionship*. Right! Who was I kidding?

The minute Weldon showed up at the door, my nervousness drained away. He was easy-going, unpretentious, and a perfect gentleman. He helped me with my jacket, opened doors for me, and held his hand at my back as we crossed streets and climbed up into the bleachers. I loved the attention. Conversation came easy and in the course of our information exchange we realized that we had graduated from high school the same year, 1956. I was in Pennsylvania; he was in West Texas. Thousands of miles apart, yet here we were sharing similar memories of the fads, music, and slang of those good old days. I had planned on skipping my Saturday night Bible Study to go on our dinner date the next night, but when I mentioned that to Weldon, he didn't want me to miss the study on his account. He suggested that we wait until Sunday and go to dinner right after church.

What a faux pas that event turned out to be! Not the dinner date, that was wonderful. We met at a little Italian Restaurant, and we were seated in a small room that we had all to ourselves. The privacy was great for getting better acquainted. It was after our meal and we had left the restaurant that things went wrong. Keep in mind that I had not dated in over forty years; I was way out of practice. We had both driven in separate vehicles since we were going to meet for dinner after the church service. Weldon walked me to my pickup and lingered while I unlocked the door. I thanked him, got in, and drove off. Only then did it dawn on me that he was standing there like he still wanted to talk. I hadn't even invited him to the house to visit awhile! It was Sunday afternoon, nothing much for either of us to do alone. Realizing my stupid blunder too late, I was sure he'd never ask me out again.

I was wrong. We talked on the phone often during that week, and the next weekend we had dinner again. This time when he brought me home I invited him in. Neither of us seemed to run out of conversation, and everything was going great. Although I was ecstatic with my new-found friend, I did not want to mislead him. I decided to express my feelings while we were sitting around my kitchen table drinking a cup of tea. There was a time when I would not have been brave enough to state my boundaries. Not this new, confident me. "I think you should know," I said, easing into my bold announcement. "I really enjoy being with you, and I love having you for a friend but I'm not ready for a serious relationship."

Weldon quickly sat back in his chair and squared his shoulders, obviously surprised by my announcement "No, I'm not either," he said.

I was relieved that we made our intentions clear. But later, lying in bed in the silent darkness, I questioned my feelings. Weldon had so many qualities that I respected and admired; I liked everything about him and it scared me. Suppose things got serious between us. Even though I felt a strong attraction to him from the moment I first saw him, I wasn't sure I'd ever be ready to go back to the routine of a constant mate again.

So much for stating boundaries! Two weeks after our conversation at the kitchen table, we were spending all our free time together. Weldon, who is a journeyman electrician, even called me on his cell phone every morning when he reached his work site—just to say good morning and talk a few minutes before getting out of his truck. When he got home at night, he'd call to say he'd be over after his shower. We would sit on the loveseat in my living room and talk for hours; some nights we didn't even bother turning on the TV. Occasionally, Weldon brought over old newspaper clippings or photo albums, and I'd get out my albums. As we shared stories of our life through pictures, we learned of each other's family history, the places we'd been, and the things we had done.

As our talks continued during those early days of dating, we discovered that we also shared the same principles, enjoyed the same music and shows, and were equally matched in our faith. Even our personalities and temperaments were alike. Sometimes our words were for the future and what we'd like to do. Always, these leisure moments were interspersed with little love gifts to each other: a kiss, a hug, a caressing hand.

One evening, Weldon gave me a shy look and said, "I've never talked this much to anyone."

That he felt this comfortable with me was a great compliment. I felt the same way. I couldn't think of anything I wouldn't want to share with him. Our favorite sharing topics were from our teen years, like the time we were coming home after an evening out and we got to talking about the silly sayings we used back in those glorious days. Weldon took a corner pretty fast and I had to grab hold of the door handle to keep from sliding across the seat.

"We called these opportunity curves," I said.

On the next sharp turn, Weldon rammed his foot on the gas pedal and this time I did slide across the seat, ending up against him. "COD," he said.

"What?"

"Come Over Darling," he answered with a deep Texas drawl and boyish grin, which had us both laughing—remember, we were two *old* folks.

From then on, this routine was repeated whenever we were driving any place. When we got carried away in teasing and playful laughter like this, I was never sure if I was with Weldon, the boy, or Weldon, the man. I've often wished that I could have known him when we were young. I would like to know what he was like back then. But that was not to be. Now is our time. And whenever that mischievous sparkle appears in his eyes, and he gets that impish grin, I am transported back to youth with him. In that fleeting moment my heart is full of joy, all of life is still ahead of us, and my hair is brown again.

Of all the joys Weldon brought to my life, I'd have to say the greatest one was this return of laughter. I'm referring to the belly-shaking, side-aching kind of laughter that makes the soul sing—something that had died in me long ago. Weldon's hardy laugh was so catchy that I couldn't resist joining in. Whenever one of us said or did something silly, we'd get caught up in a fit of uncontrolled hilarity which spewed forth with the spontaneity and energy of firecracker sparks. Happy-tears followed, cascading down my cheeks, and as soon as I wiped them away, others took their place. The only way I could stop laughing was to turn away from him until I settled down.

"I haven't laughed like this for so long that I forgot how good it feels," I told him after one of our giggle-fits.

"It's been a long time for me, too," he said, taking hold of my hand.

We had both been through hard times. The agony of watching our spouses suffer from a horrible disease and the ensuing upheaval their deaths had on our lives, was difficult beyond words. During one of our more serious talks he explained how agonizing it was to watch his wife's suffering while she was on hospice care at home. "I don't ever want to go through anything like that again," he said.

I understood exactly how he felt and the revelation was just one more thing we had in common. People who haven't been there don't understand. Full time hospice care for a loved one is exhausting and very sad, even with the help of visiting nurses. When the battle is over, guilt rushes in, making you wonder what more you could have done or what you could have done differently. Weldon didn't have to explain his feelings, I knew how he felt. Finding someone with whom we could move beyond the sadness and find laughter again was a pleasure. Weldon and I were good for each other.

10

In addition to all the other joys Weldon brought into my life, I was truly happy that he was a Christian with whom I could share my faith. Since he had to pass my house on his way to church on Sunday mornings, he began picking me up to ride with him. I loved having him sit beside me in the pew, kneeling beside him as we took communion at the altar, and listening to him sing the hymns that he knew so well. He had been raised in the church and it was obvious his faith was deep. I especially liked the way he held my hand and played with my fingers while he listened intently to the pastor's sermon. One of the most profound religious experiences we shared happened one Sunday while Weldon and I knelt at the altar rail taking communion. After we received the communion elements, he closed his hands around one of mine as they rested on the communion rail. I immediately had a powerful feeling of connection—to God, to each other—that is difficult to explain. I sensed a feeling like God was standing over us and resting His hands on our heads in a blessing. Within me, my soul stirred. The way Weldon's hands tightened on mine, I knew that he felt something, too. Back at our place in the pews, I bowed my head and closed my eyes to thank God for bringing this man of such strong faith into my life. Raising my head again, I saw that Weldon was also praying. On the way home, he told me that he thanked God for me in church that morning. He was praying the same prayer that I was praying! I can't fully understand or explain what happened that Sunday morning, but I know that something extraordinary took place.

It didn't take long for church members to start referring to us as a twosome. Different ones frequently told us what an attractive couple we made, how happy they were for us, or what an inspiration we were to them. Perhaps this happened because Weldon was always holding my hand, and I wore a perpetual smile.

"I'm glad they support us," Weldon told me. "I was afraid it was too soon after my wife's death to be with another woman."

Until I heard his words, I was not aware that he had been worried about what people would think of him dating again one year after losing his wife. He did not want anyone to think he was being disrespectful of her memory. He needed to hear that it was okay with those who had known them as a couple for twenty-seven years. God covered Weldon's fear by sending people to deliver His message that it was okay to love again.

God speaks through angels.

Even though neither of us had planned to rush into a serious relationship, that decision was out of our control. Our feelings were like run-away horses. As hard as we tried, we couldn't rein them in. I was no longer certain that I wanted to. We had now been dating steadily for a several months and we were sure that God's hand had arranged our meeting. In a world so big, only divine intervention could have brought me, not just to the same town as Weldon, but to the same street, and at a time when we were both free to be with each other. I had not been the only one being led;

God was working on Weldon, too. Years before I came on the scene, he had left the Ferris Heights Church because his wife was unhappy there. After she died, he returned—but not until one year later, after I arrived in Waxahachie and joined that church. In explaining why he came back there, he said, "Something told me that I needed to go back to that church. When I saw you walk in the room I knew that was why."

*God speaks in heart whispers (*and I'm not the only one who hears them*).*

Although we had accepted that we were meant to be together, neither of us was ready to define whether together meant life-long friends or something more. I think Weldon decided to take a step toward figuring that out one evening while he was at my house. At nine o'clock he was ready to go home; tomorrow was a work day and he had to get up at five in the morning. I walked him to the door, as always. We were standing in the foyer saying good-night, and he reached for the door knob. Before pulling the door open he did something he had not attempted until now. He turned and kissed me—twice. Then he made a hasty exit. I returned to the living room and sat on the couch wondering what in the world was happening to me. My hands were trembling and everything inside me was churning, a feeling I can only explain as the fizz in a freshly-poured soft drink. I had been kissed countless times through the years by boyfriends, husband, children, and grandchildren but I was not prepared for what this one made me feel.

I'd spent enough time with Weldon by now to know what a great guy he was and how gentle and compassionate. But now that we were getting closer, I didn't know what to think about the possibility of getting married again. I knew I had better figure that out before we went any further. God had brought me on this incredible journey and blessed me in so many ways that I did not want my feelings for Weldon to interfere with any future plans God had in store for me. When I retired that night, after the mind shattering kiss, I entered into fervent prayer with God. On this night of emotional turmoil, I desperately needed to hear Him speak. But I could not stop talking to Him about my feelings and fears, and it's not easy to hear somebody when your lips are working and your ears aren't. It wasn't until I stopped babbling and the room became silent that God's answer came as clearly as if He were standing right beside my bed. "You asked for a Christian partner; I'm answering your prayers." If I'd been hit in the face with a water balloon, I couldn't have been more stunned. After Tom died, I forgot about all the times I had asked God to help him become a Christian so we could share our faith. But God had not forgotten. God never forgets. He answered my prayers in His way and His time, and I was humbled once more to know that God loved me so much that He kept my request in his mind until the perfect time to answer it. I tucked His words in my heart for the time when they would come to be. And after that when Weldon and I were together, I felt more relaxed. God was in control and I didn't need to worry about the details.

God speaks in heart whispers (which you can only hear when you're not talking yourself).

I was thrilled that Weldon liked to get out and do things or go places, like me. No couch potato was he. We went to the movie theater, played "42" with friends, and saw several live dramas. We drove to West Texas to meet kin of Weldon's and I was mesmerized by the difference in the landscape: the big white turbines which supplied electricity, the endless cotton fields, and working oil wells all through the area. We also went to the state fair and the rodeo when they came to town. And we enjoyed going to the high school football games. Sometimes we just went out walking while holding hands. We didn't say much while we walked; we didn't have to. We found pleasure in just being together.

One day when Weldon came to pick me up, he wanted to go look at a boat that was advertised for sale. In one of our long conversations he mentioned the possibility of retiring soon and I wondered if that was on his mind when he brought up the subject of a fishing boat. As a young boy, Weldon had spent memorable times fishing with his grandfather and an uncle who was a fishing guide. He has many pictures of their fishing trips and many stories of Uncle Smokey. It was clear that fishing would be part of his retirement when it came. I, however, knew nothing about the craft. When we arrived at the place where the boat was for sale, Weldon was hooked. It became his. Of course, he couldn't wait to take me fishing. Strangely, I liked it, especially the fight in catching a fish and bringing it into the boat. But I did not like the squiggly little slimy things used for bait. Poor Weldon, I couldn't bring myself to bait my own hook or take the fish I caught off the hook. Weldon never complained about doing those things for me. He gave me lessons on casting, how deep to let my hook sink down into the water, and how to gently tug the line as soon as I felt a nibble. He was so patient, and happy to have me go fishing with him. And that made me happy.

Unfortunately, our time together wasn't all fun and games. While I was busy building a new life, my family was going through some rough times. Wendy was experiencing health problems and multiple surgeries. Though we talked often on the phone, I felt bad that I couldn't be with her. When I left San Antonio, Vicky's husband was expecting to be sent to a new duty station and she was prepared to go with him; instead, he was deployed to Iraq—three different times. Each time, she was left alone for a year to raise their daughter and take care of their home, and I was too far away to help her when she needed me most. Jeff was going through a nasty divorce and there were times when he just needed to talk to somebody and vent. As I listened to him reveal, bit by bit, his hurts and agony, my heart broke. Then Tommy suddenly moved away. Nobody from the family heard from him and the phone company had no listing in his name. I didn't know where he was, if he was all alone, or if he was well. Though I prayed for him daily, it didn't stop me from worrying. It wasn't just me having family troubles. Weldon's only child, his daughter Kelly, was going through a nasty divorce, too.

From the very first time that Weldon saw me cry he opened his arms and closed me inside, offering comforting words to take away my pain. His compassion was a soothing balm. In all the years I had spent with Tom, I fought tears. When I did cry, it was behind the closed bathroom door under the guise of a running shower, or I waited until he went to sleep and cried into my pillow. Tom was, above all else, a tough career sergeant, a role that would remain with him long after his retirement. There was no place in his world for tears. Weldon let me see that it was okay to let my vulnerability show; he would be beside me through hard times as well as happy ones. My love for him grew deeper.

Everyday life and ordinary tasks don't stop when one is preoccupied with a new beau. It was time for me to get my annual teeth cleaning and I had not found a dentist yet.

I asked Weldon if he could suggest someone, and he gave me the name of a woman who used to be a member of our church. From my first appointment, I liked her. I learned that she had been the class Sunday school teacher that I replaced. I guess gossip travels fast in small towns because she had heard that Weldon and I were dating. "That's nice. You have somebody to go out and eat with," she said.

She probably hadn't meant to confine our friendship into a package of so little significance that it only applied to eating together, but that's how I took it. I wanted to scream, "You don't understand. We're in love." I wonder why people think that when you reach a certain age you're incapable of having deep feelings anymore. As I see it, love in the senior years comes with years of maturing, of learning what we really want, and having experienced what life can throw at us. But I let her remark slide by.

While Weldon and I were paying attention to other things beside the weather, winter had slipped away. The arrival of March ushered in spring. Trees were budding; birds were coming back from their winter homes, and Weldon and I were giddy with happiness. With planting season upon us, we headed out to the nursery on a Saturday morning. I had to get plants and mulch for my flower bed, and Weldon needed starters for his vegetable garden. After parking his pickup, Weldon grabbed one of the large, flat garden carts that someone left in the parking lot—the two-deck kind with no sides. He started pushing it back to the store on our way in.

"Give me a ride," I teased.

He stopped walking and gave me one of his guarded smiles. "Get on."

I had only been kidding but now that I had an invitation, I sat atop the cart, and tucked my feet on the edge of the lower section. Chuckling to himself, Weldon started walking faster.

"Yee—Hah," I squealed, in a voice meant for Weldon only. I didn't notice if other patrons were watching us two grey-haired fools and wondering if we were two demented escapees from the local old-folks home. It didn't matter. Love is a stronger emotion than embarrassment. Nearing the entrance, I dismounted and regained my composure. We went inside and respectably walked the aisles as we made our selections, but within my chest my heart was still giggling with happiness.

That wonderful actress, Candice Bergen, once stated, "People can get crazier as they get older. I can just be weird whenever I want, and there's the freedom of not caring what people think."[3]

That's exactly how I felt; I was in no way embarrassed by our moment of gaiety. Don't get me wrong, I know there are times and places for dignity and respect but it seems to me that too many older people quit living life to the fullest just because of the numbers in their age. They become stagnant waiting for what? Death? I wish more of us could keep the child within alive.

In our continuing state of euphoria, Weldon and I sang a lot. I am not a singer, not even in the shower. But Weldon had a new Ford-150 with a great stereo system. He had loaded it with CDs and whenever one of our favorites came on, we'd join in. I'm not talking about humming or singing softly so we couldn't hear each other. Enclosed in the privacy of his truck cab, we belted out our duets as if we were performing for a full house at the Grand Ole Opry. We were having way too much fun to think about the "bump" that lay ahead.

11

I t seemed like March had barely shown her face before April had arrived at what seemed like break-neck speed. In the interim between the planning stages and the calendar appearance of my sailing date, Weldon and I had been having the time of our lives. But now, the sudden realization of being apart for two weeks had us agonizing over the separation. I didn't want to leave him, and he wasn't keen on me going off and leaving him behind. He had dropped hints that he was afraid I'd meet someone else on the cruise. I knew that wasn't going to happen, but I was worried that the special feelings we had forged might diminish after two weeks of total isolation from each other.

The evening before I left, he showed up at my door in a starched white shirt and jeans with a crease sharp enough to cut one's finger. He was carrying a florist's bouquet: one perfect red rose with sprigs of greenery and delicate baby's breath. After I thanked him with a kiss (maybe it was more than one) we ate the special dinner I had prepared. As soon as we'd finished eating and cleared away the dishes he asked, "Are you going to put on your little black dress?"

I had been telling him for weeks that I had to watch what I ate or I wouldn't fit into the "little black dress" I had bought for the cruise. When he had said that he'd like to see me in it, I promised I would model it for him before I left on the trip. Now he was holding me to that promise. "I'll model it for you if you dance with me," I teased.

"Okay," he said, with a smile and a twinkle in those gorgeous blue eyes. His answer had taken me by surprise. Probably the only thing we had never talked about was whether he liked to dance. On this night, I had a dancing partner. I lit candles around the living room and slipped some dreamy music into the CD player. Then I retreated to my bedroom where I put on the dress, black lace stockings, makeup, and jewelry, just like I'd wear them for formal occasions on the cruise. When I returned, Weldon's eyes opened wide.

"You look pretty," he said, "You always look pretty but tonight you're even better." It was the first of many times he would tell me this during the evening.

He slipped his arm around me and pulled me close. Time drifted away as we danced around the living room amid willowy shadows from the flickering candlelight. His hand caressed my back and our steps became smaller, slower. He kissed me, and my heart skipped a beat. He made me feel like a young girl again with an endless future ahead of me instead of someone whose life was already more than half-used up. I wanted to spend the rest of my days in his arms.

After a few songs, we took a break...sipped a glass of wine...made small talk. "Are you ready to dance again?" he asked, his voice low and gentle.

I was.

This pattern continued for the rest of the evening while the CDs played, but our feet and swaying bodies moved now to music that was only in our hearts. He whispered "I love you."

I echoed a response. This magical night was the most beautiful time of my life. I thought this kind of romance only happened in movies and novels. Tonight, I lived it and I will carry the memory with me forever.

The following morning, I stopped by his house on my way to the airport to say so long. He kissed me goodbye—several times. We held hands as he walked me to my pickup. When he opened the driver's side door, I didn't want to let go of him. We kissed one last time. Slowly, I slid my hand from his until only our fingertips were touching. Then they, too, broke contact. As I pulled out of the driveway he stood there watching me. Looking in my rearview mirror, my eyes were fixed on him until I had to turn the corner and couldn't see him anymore. Since meeting, we hadn't been away from each other for the length of time I would be gone. This two-week Panama Canal Cruise was to be the trip of my lifetime but as I drove away the enthusiasm I felt when my friends and I first talked about this vacation was no longer with me. Weldon's red rose from last night was pinned to the shoulder of my blouse.

The Miami Airport was bustling when my plane landed. My friends from San Antonio and my roommate from Minnesota arrived on earlier flights but none of us had trouble finding each other. We chatted excitedly while we located our baggage and boarded the bus that took us to the sea port. In spite of having to leave Weldon behind, I was drawn into my traveling partners' enthusiasm. A new adventure lay ahead and it promised to be very interesting. My mind was free of worry and I was feeling upbeat in a relaxed, carefree kind of way. Our ship, Royal Caribbean's "Radiance of the Sea," was sitting in the port when we arrived. An amazing thirteen stories high, it was a sight to behold. Before boarding, we were directed to an enormous port-side building. Inside, a long line of people was being cleared for embarkation. The four of us joined the line and as we slowly made our way through it we fidgeted with impatience and chatter. We were anxious to get on the ship and see what our home for the next fourteen days looked like. Upon making it to our cabins we found ourselves surrounded in luxury. Raye and I delighted in our room's personal balcony and wasted no time stepping out on it. Moist air swept across the ocean leaving salty vapors on our skin and invigorating our senses. A few cabins over from ours, Shirley and Jim were out on their balcony and waved to us. We were glad to discover that we could easily talk to each other from our balconies.

After checking out our cabins, all passengers had to meet on deck for instructions on how to use the life vests and where to report to the life boats in the event we should need them—a moment of reality check we had not considered. As we pulled out of Miami and headed out to sea, passengers lined the railings, waving goodbye and throwing confetti as the ship's horn sounded, loud and impressive. Excitement filled the air and our foursome was caught up in every minute of it. The water was choppy as we proceeded out of the bay; we'd be rocked to sleep on our first night out. Dinner that evening introduced us to the high-class service and scrumptious gourmet foods we would be enjoying. And no dishes to wash! We were assigned to a table with three other couples, and one's daughter. We quickly found out that they were loads of fun. We laughed and kept up a lively conversation as if we had known each other forever. We were enjoying ourselves so much that we were the last ones to leave the dining room, a habit that would become routine. After dinner we were treated to a wonderful live stage show, the first of many that would be part of our nightly entertainment. When we finally retreated to our cabin that night, I placed Weldon's rose on the nightstand beside my bed, where it was the last thing I'd see every night and the first thing every morning.

On our second day of sailing we reached the open sea, no land in sight. Finding some time alone, I went up to the top deck and found an isolated nook where I could stand at the rails and look out over the vast ocean. As far as I could see, there was nothing but water and a pristine blue sky that dipped into it at the horizon. I felt like I was looking into endless time and space, and wondered if this might be a glimpse of what the road to Heaven looks like as we leave this earthly existence and travel to eternity.

I had sought this private moment because today marked the second anniversary of Tom's death; tomorrow would have been our forty-sixth wedding anniversary. With the dates, came memories. Looking out over the water, I said a prayer for his soul to rest in peace. As though he were there in spirit, I began talking to him. I expressed remorse that we had never said a true goodbye—no *thanks for all the years together*, no *I love you*, no *I'll look for you in heaven*. I attempted a brief version of that now. I also told him about Weldon. One of the last things Tom talked about before slipping into a coma was his remorse in leaving me alone. I told him it was okay, that our kids would be there to help me if I needed anything. Now I shared with him that I was not alone; I had a wonderful new partner in my life who was very good to me. I know Tom would have liked Weldon.

As more memories of my years with Tom wove through my mind, I recalled major problems we had wrestled with and how hard they had been to work through. I wasn't aware that the heartache and anger of these problems was still buried deep within me, but God knew. His breath was all over this moment. With 2,100 passengers and a crew of 859 on board the ship there were always people walking around on the decks. Yet, during my time of introspection nobody had come through this space. It had been only God, Tom and I. That was evidence enough for me to understand that God was telling me I needed to take care of my unfinished business with Tom so I could make room in my heart for the love Weldon had for me. Tom was in a better place; I still had the rest of my life to live. I felt quiet tears trickle down my cheeks like they were washing away my hurt and anger. Through my mind's eye I imagined those bad memories falling into the ocean and being carried away on the waves never to be seen again. This simple act left me feeling refreshed and new, I had needed this closure. And I still had the good memories of our family fun times, like camping and little league games. Before getting on this ship, I had grown comfortable thinking my journey with God had reached completion: I was where He wanted me to be, I found a new life that I was ecstatic about, and I had all that I'd ever need. But after this moment on the deck with God, I suspected this trip was just a detour down a side street of our journey. He still had lessons for me. And the first one was forgiveness and acceptance.

God speaks through heart whispers.

I inhaled deeply of the clean, fresh air then turned slowly in a full circle. Overhead, a sparkling sun dangled rays that danced on the rippling ocean while 11 decks below me, the ship's engines churned a trail of aqua waves and gurgling whitecaps. The water had calmed since leaving Florida and its swishing sound, along with a gentle breeze, made pleasant companions. Lingering at the rail, I was mesmerized by the rhythm of the sea. It was one of those glad-to-be-alive-days and I felt like the luckiest person in the world to be here on the deck of this luxury liner with nothing to do for the next two weeks except relax and be pampered. I had found Utopia.

Standing in the midst of this serene splendor, I felt very near to God, as if I could reach out and touch Him. I marveled anew at how far He had brought me in the past two years and how much our journey together had deepened my relationship with Him. It occurred to me that God and I had never celebrated this milestone. Enveloped in this special moment I longed to do that. Happiness flowed like music through my veins, and my heart was a bright party-balloon filled to capacity with love and gratitude. I wanted to hug Him, to sing and frolic with Him. Maybe one day I will be able to do that. But for now, I was ready to get back to my travel mates.

Our little group of four turned out to be quite compatible. We enjoyed the daily activities on board, going to the nightly shows, sunbathing on lounge chairs, feasting on the fabulous food, and alternating visits between Shirley and Jim's balcony and ours every evening for chitchat and a before-dinner cocktail. Those balcony visits became a highlight of our days. Though we spent mornings and afternoons exploring and attending activities we eagerly looked forward to our private pre-dinner time to relax and just be ourselves. Being with old friends again felt great. My one disappointment was not being able to communicate with Weldon. My cell phone wouldn't work at sea. I tried numerous times to e-mail him from the computer room onboard but for some reason the ship was having difficulty picking up a signal and couldn't send off transmissions.

As the days rolled by, we stopped at many ports. I learned much about the different characteristics of cre-ation, and people of varying cultures and mind-sets. Every port, it seemed, had a new lesson to learn. Our first stop was Aruba, an island once buried underwater. Over the years, its black lava spewed from many volcanic eruptions and added to the surface until the mass was tall enough to rise out of the ocean. It felt pretty awesome to be walking on land that at one time wasn't even known to be here. Houses were colorful and quaint but the land was dark with many lava deposits. The island's motto, "One Friendly Island," was well suited to the citizens; everyone we encountered was cheerful and friendly; nobody was in a rush. I won-dered how a whole island's population managed to stay so motivated and why life couldn't be like this all over the world. I bought a tee shirt with the Island's motto on it for Weldon. While we were in the shopping district my friends and I looked for a post office so I could send mail I had written to Weldon. We found one in a little out-of-the-way place. I was shocked to learn how high postage rates were in other countries. Two post cards and a letter cost me $5.85, and the postal clerk said I'd probably get home before my mail arrived.

It took five days to reach the main attraction of our trip: the famous Panama Canal. As with every other port stop we made, we were directed to the ship's theater the night before to be briefed on what to expect. The tour director explained that in order for ships to have a direct passage between the Atlantic and Pacific Oceans, a canal had to be cut through the land connecting North and South America. Since the ocean was much deeper than the canal, ships had to be raised up in order to pass over this section of land. This was accomplished by the *locks*. It took many men working for a long period of time to build the locks. The magnitude of the process was mind-boggling to me. I was bursting with eagerness to observe the miraculous process of passing through them.

Early the next morning, Raye and I hurried to find a good lookout spot on the upper decks. Hundreds of others had beaten us there. Crew members and passengers alike were crammed together along the rails, but we found a high spot where we could see over the crowd. I hadn't quite pictured in my mind how the locks were going to work. Nothing could have prepared me for the phenomenal event that we experienced. Our ship entered a huge box-like structure with tall concrete walls at each side of the ship and a concrete gate in front of it. Once inside, a gate closed behind us. Water was released into the enclosure, and our massive ship rose slowly on the water with the ease of a rubber tub toy. We watched our ascent on depth-level markers along the concrete walls. Reaching the top of that level, the gates in front opened and we passed through to another lock. Finally, we were high enough to cross over the ten-mile-wide portion of land that was now covered by Gaton Lake. Upon crossing the lake, we had to go though another set of locks to be lowered into the Pacific Ocean.

This slow process had taken most of the day with the temperature reaching a blazing 106 degrees in the shade but passing through the locks was so mesmerizing that most onlookers hadn't left the deck to go inside to the cool air-conditioning. I wished Weldon, my kids, and grandkids could have been there to experience this once-in-a-life-time experience with me. Even with the dozens of pictures I took I knew I could never do justice to this event. At the beginning of the cruise I was moved by the wonder of nature as I viewed it from the endless expanse of the sea. Now my mind was boggled by the magnificence of the canal passage, the intelligence of men, and the strength, courage, and faith it took to create the canal and the locks that brought ship traffic through it. It was, to say the least, a very humbling experience.

That evening, we docked at Fuerte Amador, Panama. For the first time I missed the ship's nightly show because I was too antsy to sit through it. I was miserably lone-some for Weldon and wished we could at least communi-cate with each other. In the computer room, I tried again to e-mail him — still no signal. At this point, I wondered if God had given us this total separation for me to decide if I really wanted another life-partner, or if He wanted me to realize how much better my life had become since Weldon entered in. Perhaps it was a little of both.

12

Saturday was another sail day in the open sea so we ladies decided to pamper ourselves, starting with breakfast in bed. Next, leaving Jim behind, we had a make-over and went shopping in the ship's mall where we tried on clothes and jewelry just for fun. We watched an ice-carving demonstration at poolside, and tried our luck at the casino. Girlfriend times are always fun. Jim rejoined us for the second formal dinner and stage show that evening. He was such a good sport about traveling with three women whom we jokingly referred to as his "harem." He never seemed uncomfortable about being outnumbered, and we thoroughly enjoyed having him with us.

Sunday marked one week of sailing. Raye and I were up early. Looking out the balcony door, we discovered that we had docked at Calderas, Costa Rico during the night.

We had scheduled a tour to a rain forest here, something I had always wanted to see so I was anxious to get going. As our bus drove to the forest we saw that this area of the country—about one hundred feet of coastline along the Pacific Ocean –was very underprivileged. Homes were ramshackle buildings with no windows or doors. Our guide provided much information about the country and its people. He passed out some examples of native products, including cocoa beans, and we quickly learned what a comedian he was when he described them.

"The gel-like substance covering the beans," he said, "causes diarrhea. When I was in high school I got a job picking cocoa beans. I was new and inexperienced so when the workers told me my job was to suck off the gel, then spit out the seeds to be crushed into the chocolate powder I did. And I was number-two ugly all day long!"

In spite of the humble living, the citizens were very ecology-minded and took pride in protecting plants and animal life, something we realized while standing at the entry to the forest waiting for the cable cars that would carry us to the highest point. A small sign at ground level said *Caution, Ant Crossing*. Looking more closely, I saw a long line of the tiny creatures traveling from one side of the walkway to the other. Our cable-car attendant warned approaching customers not to step on the ants.

"Each creature has its part in keeping the balance of nature," she said, making it evident that the people of Calderas were far more appreciative of God's creation than most Americans.

The cable-cars had roofs but were open along the sides so we could see clearly and hear every minute sound. We started our ascent, and as though they were cued, passengers—eight to a car—fell silent in fear of disrupting the magic of this place. As our cars crept along the cables into the thicket my ears picked up echoes of melodic bird calls, the occasional rustle of leaves as birds or slight breezes moved through them, and the delicate trickle of small waterfalls far below us. The thick foliage rose far above us. Everything looked spotlessly clean and untouched, and our heads turned side-to-side, up-and-down, as we tried to take it all in. With our eyes glued to the trees and vines, we spotted a colorful Toucan, a white-faced monkey, a huge, pale-blue butterfly among many other species, and a striking scarlet Macaw.

Back on the ground, our tour ended with a walk along the floor of the forest. Our guide stopped by a tree with wide, flat roots growing above ground. He stooped and smacked his palms rhythmically against the hollow roots and explained that natives from long ago used this method to send messages to one another.

"The sound can be heard for two miles in the forest," he said.

I wondered if those natives would be as confused and overwhelmed as I was with the abundance of technological communication gadgets that we have in 2011. I stopped to gaze up toward the sky but the towering trees were spread out in such a thick canopy of foliage that I could not see through the tops of them.

As a child living in a small coal-mining town in a valley of Pennsylvania's mountains I could stand in my back yard, turn in a circle, and see mountains all around. Some were closer than others but there was no break in them. I remember thinking that those mountains were the edge of the world and imagined there was nothing but empty space beyond them. Years later, I married an Air Force career man and lived in many places whenever he was sent to a new duty station, including a year in Europe. Though I'd seen a much broader view of the world my viewpoint here in the forest made me realize how truly infinite earth was. I felt like a mere speck in the grand scheme of Creation. Visiting the forest was an astounding experience: the beauty, the majesty, the purity and wonder of it was something I would remember always.

Three days later, we pulled into the port of Huatulco, Mexico. Here, our group of four had chosen a land tour to visit actual homes of the natives and learn about their towns and traditions. Our tour guide loaded us in a van with six other people and off we went. Our first stop was in a primitive dwelling with dirt floors and gaping openings in the walls in place of windows and doors. The matron of the house, a tiny, wrinkled old woman, looked like she'd never had a full belly or an easy day. She proudly demonstrated how she made cornmeal from ground corn and water, slapping the thickened mixture back and forth between her small hands that were bony and worn. After she flattened the cornmeal into tortillas she threw them on her ancient stove—the only object in her kitchen. As she turned them over with her hands, her fingers never flinched from the heat. She had so little, yet she smiled with pride as she passed out her delicious tortillas for our group to taste.

Leaving there, we went to a cactus farm where the owner wore a constant grin. He explained that cactus, which grew abundantly on his dry, parched land, was used for food and medicinal purposes. Using his sharp knife (most men here carried machetes), he demonstrated how to shave off the thorns which made the cactus edible. His family had set up a large outdoor table to serve us cactus salad to which tomatoes, onion and garlic had been added. I was hesitant about the thought of eating cactus but pleasantly surprised by the sweet taste. Served on fresh tortillas then washed down with bottled water supplied by the tour company, the cactus salad made a tasty lunch. The people we'd seen so far may have been poor in our eyes but they didn't lack in resourcefulness or generosity. This man had only cactus but he knew how to use it well. Incidentally, his name was José and his wife's was Maria, which in English translates to Joseph and Mary.

Next on the agenda was a tangerine farm where our translator Erica interpreted the owner's conversation for us. "The land has been in his family for many years. Generations of men have nourished the orchard, tilling the soil with primitive hand tools and planting each tree from seed." She paused to get his next words before continuing, obviously new at this job but doing her best. "They have always sold the fruit as their means of living. Now the market has become too competitive and they can barely survive by selling only locally."

I noticed how hard and flaky the ground was and the number of tangerines drying up and dying on the trees but the family's strong spirit was obvious. "They are presently attempting to build an irrigation system for their orchard," said Erica. "They must dig down thirty feet to reach water. So far, they have reached only nine feet—all with hand tools."

Then she pointed out *Black Trees* growing in the same orchard. "It is believed their leaves contain antibiotics that provide rapid healing. The workers cut their fingers often while harvesting the fruit; they press the leaves of this tree to their open cuts so they will heal."

I thought of our modern hospitals and numerous out-patient clinics, our green lawns and sprinkler systems, our modern technology, and suddenly felt very spoiled and somewhat embarrassed over the excesses in my life that were just for pleasure and not need.

The next family we saw showed us quite a different scene. A young man, who looked like he was in his late teens, was making bricks by mixing clay-like dirt and water with his bare feet. He formed the bricks by packing the muddy mixture into wooden molds then gently turned the mold over on the ground. Next, he lifted off the mold to let the bricks dry and harden.

"They must dry in the sun for two days," he said. Then he explained that his family sells the bricks for fifty cents each. However, he was making them for his own use. According to custom, when a young couple wishes to marry the boy's father builds the basis for a hut—four poles with a palm-leaf roof. The groom-to-be has to build the walls out of the clay bricks. The couple cannot marry until the walls are built. The floors will remain uncovered dirt and there will be no windows or doors, like all homes here. I thought of the first apartment I lived in when I married. It was located above a store and I had to climb a long flight of steps to go in and out. Suddenly, it didn't seem so small and inadequate.

Finally, our group explored the downtown area of Huatulco. It was old, but colorful, and the atmosphere was more cheerful than in the villages. We wandered through a beautiful little church with white stucco walls and sparse but beautiful religious items for use in worship. It was an immaculate place that looked like everything, including the pews, was handmade by very skilled people. The natives who had so little for themselves obviously gave first—and their best—to God. It said much for their faith. In spite of the harsh living I'd witnessed here I loved Huatulco. The people were humble and friendly, and they showed me much about courage, strength, and determination. In comparison to life in America, they appeared to be under-privileged but they were rich in many ways and they were content. Visiting here was a true lesson in trusting God to provide all we need. His loving care was very evident. Remembering how I worried about money after Tom's death I felt ashamed. This whole day's excursion opened my eyes to the hard, rugged living of many people. It also revealed their unfaltering strength and gratitude for what they had. A life so different from what most of us know can be comfortable living for others. As a writer, I am always hungry for new experiences that will provide me with knowledge I can turn into written words. But some learning is so humbling there are no words to explain it. You only feel it in your soul and hope you can become a better person because of what you learned.

Sometimes God speaks loudest through images.

Before leaving Huatulco I took off my shoes and waded knee-deep in the Pacific Ocean, which was a gorgeous blue color. I knew I probably wouldn't be this close to Pacific waters again. On our way back to the ship we passed a residential area and I asked Erica about a large building under construction that was more modern than others in the area.

"That is a *condom*," she said, and my soul smiled. I knew she meant *condominium*.

The last two port visits for our cruise were Acapulco and Cabo San Lucas, modern cities with high-rise buildings, bustling traffic, and shops lined shoulder-to-shoulder. The tour buses here were big and modern, and as we rode up into the hills and away from the cities the atmosphere spoke of magnificence and luxury. We passed impeccably manicured golf courses and elaborate hotels, and our guide pointed out the palatial mansions of John Wayne, Sylvester Stallone, Liz Taylor, and other famous movie stars. He also told us of the high-tech security and walls needed to protect their privacy. I wondered if such living was worth the price they paid and if their lives were as content as the humble people of Huatulco. Our bus parked at a high-class restaurant with elaborate flower gardens and majestic outside décor, including an eternity swimming pool that seemed to empty over the cliffs. We were allowed to walk around and enjoy the luxuries of the property or sit by the pool. I was awed by the post-card-pretty views of the ocean from high on the rugged cliffs.

With all our port stops behind us we turned our concentration to activities on board. One afternoon Shirley and Raye decided to go to a napkin-folding exhibition. I passed on that. Instead, I fixed myself a bowl of soft ice-cream and carried it out to the Sea View Café at the back end of the ship away from the wind. It was a relaxing place to sit in solace for awhile. Mesmerized by the melody of the churning waters, I reflected on how this cruise had been all I could hope for. Once again, I had to admit that my friends were right; I had been through a couple rough years and what better place to get re-charged than out on the sea isolated from life's everyday busyness. Even though I wasn't aware that I needed it, this trip had been a perfect reprieve. It was both pleasure and a learning experience; I had laughed and I had been struck silent with amazement; the people and places we visited touched my heart; my traveling companions were the best; and the live shows every night never failed to entertain us. Thankfully, we had been blessed with beautiful weather except for one day that had been overcast and windy, causing angry-looking waves. The sea was quite intimidating in gloomy weather. Mostly we enjoyed glorious sun and gentle breezes. We couldn't ask for anything more. Yet, the magic of being at sea was diminishing for me. I was ready to go home.

I missed Weldon terribly. When I was married to Tom, the military moved us often and I missed my family of origin, especially when my mom wasn't around to give me advice on caring for my newborn babies. Then there were times when Tom went TDY (temporary duty) where he'd be gone up to a week or PCS (permanent change of station) on a one-year isolated tour, and the children and I couldn't accompany him. I missed his presence at those times but I knew when I married him what I was getting into and accepted his absences as part of our lifestyle. When my children grew up and began leaving home, my heart broke a little with each of their departures. But I lived with it because mothers know the day will come when their offspring need to follow their dreams and become independent adults. What I was feeling for Weldon didn't fit into any of those categories, nor did it feel anything like those events. Finding him was like finding a part of me that had been missing for a long time. When I was with him I felt different. I was different—more alive, more like my true self. Two weeks was a long time to be apart. I yearned to be with him again. One more day of cruising, and we'd dock in San Diego, California, where I'd say goodbye to my traveling companions then catch a flight back to Texas. I hoped that nothing had changed for Weldon and me in our long absence from each other.

13

When I pulled up in front of my house in Waxahachie, Lori's car was sitting by the curb. I immediately thought there must be trouble. I didn't see any other reason why she would be waiting here for me when she didn't know what time I would arrive home. When I entered the foyer, I saw her standing in the kitchen so I walked over to her and immediately started crying. I couldn't stop as I looked all around.

"Mom, don't cry she said; I can put it all back like it was."

"No," I sobbed, trying to get control of myself so I could talk. "It's gorgeous."

"Do you really like it?" she asked.

"I love it," I said, still trying to pull myself together. Then I gave her a big hug before taking another look around my new kitchen. "Thank you so much. I can't believe you did all this in the short time I was gone."

When I moved into this house I had casually mentioned that I'd love to have a Tuscan style kitchen. Lori never said anything to me about that but while I was gone she took it upon herself to paint the entire kitchen in what she described as a faux plaster look. She had even painted several dark red bricks in random areas to look like the plaster had fallen off, as is often seen in old Tuscan homes. The background paint was a mixture of soft gold and pale tans that make a great compliment to my red canisters and other red accents. Those same colors are in a painting of a Tuscan scene that hangs in my living room.

As I turned to take in all sides of the kitchen I noticed that she had also painted a border of large white stones around the arch between the kitchen and foyer to make it look like an old stone archway. She topped all that artwork off by draping a long piece of greenery above the large bay window and hanging bunches of imitation grapes among the leaves. Each grape has a tiny light bulb inside. When I plug them in, my kitchen is transformed into a cozy Tuscan inn atmosphere. Her work was so professional and beautiful that I could not believe she accomplished all this without a helper. I was beyond overwhelmed with her generous gift, and for finding another way to make my little house uniquely mine. I hope to live here for the rest of my days.

That evening, Weldon came over as soon as he got out of work. We were both thrilled to be with each other again but once the enthusiastic welcome was over I couldn't help noticing that he seemed quieter than usual. As I suspected, the problem was the lack of communication while I was gone. Rightly, he felt ignored.

"Didn't you get any of my mail?" I asked.

"No, I didn't get mail, a phone call, or anything."

"There's no way to mail letters from the ship but I mailed you post cards and a letter from the first port stop we had. The postal clerk didn't know when they would reach you but she did say I'd probably get home before my mail did." He listened patiently as I explained that neither my cell phone nor the computer onboard the ship worked.

"I thought you forgot about me," he said.

"No way," I assured him. Now that he felt better, I couldn't stop talking about my trip. I wanted to share every moment with him. "I took lots of pictures so when they're developed we can look at them together and you can get a better idea of all these places I'm rattling on about."

"I've never been on a cruise. I want you to go on one with me," he said.

I was in no hurry to be out at sea again but the idea of going with Weldon was enticing. "Okay, but we'll have to wait until I am able to save up some money."

"This one's on me," he said, with a smile as generous as his offer.

We decided that it would be fun to go on a Christmas cruise to the Caribbean. When I called the travel agent the next day, she said it would be bad to go over the holidays. "Kids are out of school for the Christmas break and many families take vacations then. The cruise lines raise their prices because they know they'll be booking large crowds no matter what the cost is. Why don't you go right before Christmas, or right after, when they've gone back to the original cost? The Christmas trees and holiday decorations will still be hanging throughout the ships," she added.

So I chose the first week in December, eight months away.

In the meantime, Weldon's conversations kept coming back to the subject of retiring. He'd been having shoulder pain for some time and it was getting worse. Before I met him, I had never understood the harsh physical strain of being a commercial electrician. Years of lugging around heavy reels of wiring then pulling it through PVC pipe, digging trenches to bury the pipes in the ground, and carrying around ten-feet-long ladders to reach the crawl spaces of tall commercial buildings to install wiring was very strenuous on the shoulder joints. After thirty plus years of doing this, it's no wonder his body was protesting. I tried to talk him into seeing an orthopedic doctor to have it checked, but he wanted to wait until he retired, which made me think he was ready to pick a date to do that soon. However, I could see that the idea of having no job made him nervous.

"I retired once before but six months later I went back to work."

"Was it because you needed the money," I asked.

He shook his head *yes* in answer. I suspected that his wife's cancer treatments and medications were part of the reason for that. I didn't question the subject any further.

As we continued to talk, I learned that he was also concerned about what he would do with the free time if he quit working. Aware of the struggle he was having with his decision, I tried to encourage him, reminding him that we could spend more time together and go fishing, travel, or whatever we pleased. "And you'd have more time to do repairs and maintenance on your house," I added.

As we continued to explore the possibility of his retirement, it became evident that there was an underlying implication to our talks besides how he'd be spending his free time. The subject of retirement had us dancing around the "M" word without actually mentioning it. Ever since we met, it was evident to both of us that whatever was left of our lives we wanted to spend it together. Whether that meant getting married remained to be seen. Maybe we were afraid of upsetting the comfort zone we were in with just being good friends. To be honest, I wasn't sure I was ready to go through another big lifestyle adjustment after recently going through a major move. But I did love Weldon enough to commit the rest of my days to him. Besides, there was that nighttime conversation I had with God when He told me that Weldon was the answer to my prayers for a Christian mate. Making a commitment beyond being friends was a lot for both of us to think about.

Getting married in the senior years is very different from what young couples face. And my long connection to military life was another big issue to consider. For instance, one of my major concerns was how remarriage would affect my monthly government check. Tom had spent twenty two years in the Air Force, then transferred his time and benefits from that commitment to a civil service job at an Army Base where he worked another fifteen years. If I married a non-military retiree, I didn't know how it might affect the survivor benefit check I received from Tom's annuity. My social security was a mere pittance that wouldn't get me far if I lost that survivor's benefit check. Granted, getting married would mean I'd have a spouse to help me out, but if Weldon retired and no longer had his weekly salary he'd be in the same situation as I, and he had his own expenses to worry about. Many older couples who marry have to share expenses in order to be able to pay the bills. Where a younger couple might consider re-entering the work force if they got in a bind, Weldon and I were too old to do that.

Curious about what lay ahead *if* we did marry, I decided to go on an information-gathering binge making phone calls and visiting local offices during the hours that Weldon was at work. Each evening, I shared with him what I had learned.

I breathed a huge sigh of relief when I heard that my survivor's benefit check would continue unaltered if I remarried, and I would continue to get it every month until I died. However, I'd have to turn in my military ID card. I would no longer be eligible to enter military bases to shop for groceries and clothing (tax-free), or use any of the facilities and services, including the hospital clinic and legal office—things I had been doing since I was a twenty-year old bride. Still, I felt that was fair since I would no longer be the dependent of a government retiree.

My next inquiry brought a devastating blow. I learned that I would lose my government-provided Tricare Health Insurance if I married again. All my medical and surgical care plus medications were covered on this policy, also until my death. Tom and I had paid premiums on that policy until reaching the age of sixty-five at which time we no longer had to pay that fee. Losing that benefit would really put a hole in my pocket. Though I was in good health I could not depend on it staying that way with my increasing years. When I bought my house in Waxahachie, I had carefully considered my other expenses and how much I could do on my budget. If I had to buy civilian health insurance now, which is very expensive and confusing to someone who had never dealt with it, I might not be able to afford my house payment.

And speaking of houses, we each owned the homes we lived in and we both planned to leave them to our children when we died—a thought that would never enter a young, about-to-be-married couple's mind. I wasn't eager to leave my house; I was still enjoying the newness and décor that I had worked on so diligently. Luckily, Weldon already had an answer to the house situation. The night we were discussing it, he said, "I thought if I ever married again, and my wife had a home, I'd move into hers and rent mine to have more income." That sounded good to me. Besides, mine was smaller and easier to take care of and being new it wouldn't need repairs for awhile. His was over thirty years old and beginning to have problems.

Then there was the subject of burial plots—a morbid but necessary topic. All older couples should face this during the marriage-decision period to prevent a crisis when one of them passes away. Weldon owned a lot beside his prior wife. I was to be buried in Tom's grave at the Fort Sam Houston National Cemetery where the graves there are made large enough for two people, the military person and his wife or child. Again, this was something I had to clarify with the government. If I lost that privilege, my finances weren't elastic enough at this stage to include buying a cemetery plot. A call to the cemetery office verified that as long as I was married to Tom at the time of his death my eligibility to be buried with him would remain intact even if I remarried.

Some things I learned made me think maybe marriage wasn't a good idea, other times I felt like we had all the bases covered. This uncertainty made it harder to decide if I really wanted to marry again at my age. I continued to forge forward knowing that if we just decided to stay friends without marriage that would be okay too.

I knew that a good place to air out my concerns was at one of my Ditto Daughters meetings. These ladies would give me an honest opinion and the conversation would not leave the room.

"Why don't you just move in together and not worry about getting married," Dee suggested.

I'd been hearing more and more about couples our age doing this. Though cohabitation outside of marriage would be an easy solution, I didn't feel comfortable with it.

"Have you talked to my husband about this?" Janie, the pastor's wife, asked. "I'm sure he'd be willing to have a private ceremony with the two of you to ask God's blessings on your union. Having God's approval would put your mind at ease."

I had not talked to Pastor John. Nor did I plan to until I was sure where Weldon and I were headed. As I said, we had only hinted at the possibility of getting married.

As I continued my information gathering, I learned that co-habitation was quite common among older people. They were doing it for one reason: they couldn't afford the financial hardships they would endure if they married. A vivid example of this was something I learned at the tax office. If Weldon and I married we would have to pay more to the IRS than if we stayed single. That made no sense to me.

"You'd be better off if you just lived together," said the CPA who worked there. I was beginning to see why this option was gaining so much approval among elderly people.

After gathering all this information and figuring out we could live with the options facing us, Weldon asked me to marry him.

Of course, I said yes. Well, it was more like, "Yes! Yes! Yes!"

Since we both had experienced all the hoopla of formal weddings in our prior marriages, we just wanted a simple ceremony this time. Now that we were actually working toward a wedding date, Weldon made up his mind to retire on the last day of December so we could spend more time together as husband and wife. He informed his boss of this decision, and upon making this commitment, we were anxious to move forward with wedding plans.

Even though we wanted to keep the ceremony simple, a new frenzy was brought into our lives. With the December cruise we had planned earlier in the year, I romanticized about a simple exchange of vows on the ship's deck during a beautiful sunset, with the Captain officiating. We wouldn't tell friends or family about our marriage until we returned home. But when I asked our travel agent to find out if the Captain would marry us, I was flabbergasted with her return phone call.

"Their wedding package includes a reception with your friends onboard the ship before it sails, but they would have to leave before the scheduled cruise passengers boarded. It also includes a video of the ceremony, the use of a wedding hostess, flowers…"

My mind spun as she rattled on, quoting a price that was even higher than the cost of our cruise tickets. "Wait," I said. "We don't know anyone near the port who could come for a reception. All we wanted was to have the Captain exchange our vows with us."

"Well, this is the only wedding package they offer," she said, her voice deflated, as if I had just burst her bubble. I wondered if she was planning her marriage or mine.

Disappointed, I scratched the romantic wedding at sea off my list. On to option two: our church had a beautiful prayer garden. We decided to ask the Pastor to marry us there in a simple, private ceremony with just the three of us: Pastor John, Weldon, and me. Then we thought about our kids. If we were going to get married in Waxahachie, we should probably invite them or there would be hurt feelings. With this new plan, I thought about asking Dee Taylor to sing a solo to make the event a little more special, but I couldn't ask Dee without inviting the rest of my Ditto Daughters group. Now we got into the problem of working around everyone's schedule. Deciding who we'd invite and trying to keep the numbers manageable quickly got out of control. We ditched this option, too.

Option three. With Thanksgiving weekend approaching, we decided to get married that Sunday following the morning worship service, a plan that was simple, quick, easy — and legal. And being in God's house we would have His blessing. Our Christmas cruise would now be our honeymoon cruise.

Now I was ready to talk to Pastor John, who had some great advice for me. He gave me three rules to follow:

Never say should. Know what you will do and won't do — and do it!

If you react to something with Weldon, stop and ask, "Is this Tom or Weldon I'm reacting to?" In other words, don't bring baggage from past marriage into this relationship.

You can't say hello to a new life until you've said goodbye to the old one. I had already done that on my cruise.

Our big day worked out splendidly. Granddaughter Christi spent the night before the wedding at my house and she woke me at 5:00 am! We ate a hasty breakfast before she helped me get into my linen suit with a long skirt and exquisite embroidery on the jacket. Then she lovingly tucked a sprig of baby's breath in my hair and anchored it with a delicate white butterfly barrette.

Most of our church family stayed after the morning worship service to see our wedding. Jeff and Lori came there with their families, and so did Weldon's sister, a brother, and sister-in-law. Unfortunately, Kelly awoke with a stomach virus that morning and was too sick to make it to her dad's wedding. Shirley and Jim were returning from a visit to their son's house and since they had to travel IH-35 they stopped at the church to share this event with us. My writer friend from Flower Mound also surprised

EPILOGUE

My journey with God brought me to an unexpected and very different new life. As I look back, the magnitude of this experience boggles my mind. I've learned that when you walk with God the journey never ends nor does the learning stop. I assume He will take me on more adventures before I leave Earth, but this one has been the biggest and most-altering one that I've had to date. I've encountered many angels along the way, and I have grown to know God on a much more intimate basis. I've gained more wisdom about life and doing things on my own. Most surprising, I've come to know myself better. I am comfortable with who I am now, which is something I've never been able to accomplish in my many years before this time. I feel like I'm beginning to be the kind of person God intended me to be instead of the one I thought I had to be in order to please others. That's a good feeling.

Listening to God's call when I woke that morning ready to sell my house in San Antonio was a challenge that I'm glad I accepted. Such a calling can be scary. It can make you doubt whether you are truly hearing God or just responding to your own desires. When my friend in San Antonio asked how I know when God speaks to me, I couldn't explain it to her. If anyone were to ask now, I definitely have an answer.

- God speaks through heart whispers – in broad daylight or in the middle of the night.
- God speaks through angels – some are strangers, some are people we know.
- God speaks through written words – Scripture, letters, newspapers.
- God speaks in many languages – Even though we don't understand the words, the message translates itself in our heart.
- God speaks through music – like the feeling you get when you hear or sing a favorite hymn.

- God speaks through unexpected things, like a name – my two Dee Taylors: one in San Antonio, one in Waxahachie.
- God speaks through images – like the people whose lives I experienced on my Panama Canal cruise.

Even when we're sure we've heard God's voice, going where He calls us—whether it is another location or just a different phase in our life—is not easy. Sacrifice is often involved. For me, it was leaving my friends, two daughters, and everything familiar to travel into the unknown. Not everyone is called to do something that drastic, but once you've determined that God is speaking you need to trust Him in whatever He asks you to do. I once received an e-mail that offered commendable advice on this subject. It read, "Do not ask the Lord to guide your footsteps if you are not willing to move your feet." To that I add an Amen.

I often pondered the story of the disciples in Mark 1:16-18: *As Jesus walked beside the Sea of Galilee, he saw Simon and his brother Andrew casting a net into the lake, for they were fishermen. "Come, follow me," Jesus said, "and I will make you fishers of men." At once, they left their nets and followed him.*

My thoughts on this scripture always ended on the same conclusion: I could not simply walk away from life as I knew it, to follow God's calling—until I did it. Granted, my situation was not as righteous as what Simon and Andrew were being asked. However, it involved the same sacrifice, to walk away from my home and the life I had and go where I felt God was leading me. It was a huge step but I've never regretted it. I am rich with the blessings that have been given me because I made that choice.

I would be remiss not to add a warning here. If you travel with God and He showers his grace and gifts upon you, it does not mean you will be immune to troubles. Life happens. Fate throws curves. Weldon and I have faced some rough times and painful crises in our time together. He has had two major surgeries (one of them to fix his shoulder), I had a minor stroke, I was involved in a ghastly four-vehicle traffic accident that miraculously didn't kill anyone, and we both endured the agony of watching helplessly as three of our six children suffered through nasty, drawn-out divorces. God does not make these things happen to keep us on our toes; God is with us through our heartaches to keep us on our feet. And we'd surely crumble without Him.

Take notice, too, of a pattern that unfolded in my journey. I received God's help, and then I was called to serve as a Sunday school teacher, a volunteer at the child abuse center, and to write a monthly devotional column for our church newsletter. Matthew 10:8 says *"Freely you have received, freely give."* Serving others in exchange for what I'd been given was my response to the gifts I received. I've talked to many people who struggle with the serving concept because they can't figure out what they are able to do. Most are especially nervous about the idea of talking before groups but there are many other ways to be servants for Christ. Each of us is blessed with different talents and our potential to use them is incalculable, yet they are wasted if we're too paralyzed by our insecurities to go for it and trust God for assistance. Philippians 2:13 gives an assuring response to that: *"for it is God who works in you to will and to act according to his good purpose."*

When I became willing to give-back for what I received, God empowered me to do what I needed to do, just as that

Bible verse says. He never let me down, I've never crashed or become a bumbling idiot in front of groups I gave talks to, and I've had tremendous feedback on my writings. Learning to serve others means acting like God's giving to us. The difference is that in human relationships each partner expects something in return. God doesn't expect pay-back but it makes him very happy if we pass it on by serving others. If you are able, one option I would suggest is doing volunteer work. No special skills are needed and it means so much to those you serve.

After experiencing my journey, I strongly suggest to those who have lost a spouse that you do not quit living because your partner has died. You've taken care of your children, your spouse, and probably your parents, now do the same for yourself. Whether that includes pursuing an unfulfilled goal, moving to another location, learning a new skill or sport, traveling to dreamed-of places, or opening your heart to new love, is up to you. The world is a vast place full of knowledge, discoveries, and entertainment, and it's your world.

Don't get discouraged if things don't go as you anticipated. God has you covered with His plans for you. Look at my situation: when I left San Antonio my mindset was to find a small, comfortable home where I could be close to my children and grandchildren and, hopefully, stay independent as I lived out my remaining days. To put it more bluntly, I came here to die. Several acquaintances had died the same year as Tom so I was feeling vulnerable. For awhile being around family was wonderful. Then, for financial reasons, Lori had to join the work force after being a stay-at-home mom for many years. She works twelve-hour shifts as a ward clerk in a hospital. On her days off, she stays busy doing housework, shopping, or chauffeuring her youngest daughter to events. This leaves little time for her and me to get together but we talk on the phone whenever we can. Her middle daughter, Amanda, is away at college now. Christi, the one who stayed with me the summer after her papa died, graduated with a Bachelor's Degree in Science of Nursing, Registered Nurse (BSN RN) in 2006. She got married and has two little boys. She is now studying to get a Master's Degree in Science of Nursing for Family Nurse Practitioner (MSN FNP). With her hectic life, she's too busy to visit Grandma.

Jeff got a major promotion at work and I'm very proud of him. He was ecstatic to have his hard labors recognized after many years with the company and to receive a much-needed boost in pay, but he was also sad that his dad didn't live to see it happen. Now he is busy traveling around the country to check on other branches of his company or fix problems. On the weeks he isn't flying out of town, he has custody of his two children and tries to spend quality time with them while trying to get them back and forth to school and activities (his ex moved them to another school district). I rarely see his children, my grandchildren. Divorce drastically changes the lives not just of the couple and their children but of the secondary family members, too.

Vicky's husband retired from the Air Force and they moved to Phoenix, New York. She misses Texas and the family but she's trying hard to make a new life there. We try to stay connected through e-mails.

Wendy, the one I left behind in Poth, Texas, when I moved up here, continues to have constant health issues. In addition to that challenge she works full time in a hospital as the night shift R.N. It's hard for her to get away, and Waxahachie is a long distance from Poth. We rarely see each other but she calls often and we have long conversations which makes me feel close to her.

God had all those setbacks covered. Though I don't see my family as much as I hoped, He gave me Weldon to make my life full and keep me happy. I also received another wonderful surprise, I was reunited with Tommy. Before his dad died and was in the final stages of cancer, Tommy took leave from his job and came to stay with us. He was a tremendous help during that time. I sometimes had to wake him in the middle of the night to help me lift his dad or change his position. Cancer had involved Tom's bones, making his legs useless and he was too heavy for me to lift on my own. Tommy also helped the hospice orderly bathe Tom and he helped me with the wheelchair and oxygen tank when we had to go to the hospital for chemo therapy. When the cancer worsened to a point that Tom became incontinent, Tommy even helped clean up the messy accidents. He was eager to do anything to help his dad. Being with us twenty-four hours a day, our son experienced first hand the ugliness and humiliation cancer had bestowed upon his dad, a man he always knew as being strong and tough. Vicky, too, helped out a lot since she lived close by and could visit often. She always met us at the hospital when Tom had to go in for chemo treatments, but she had a husband and daughter to care for so I was glad to have Tommy with us day and night.

Although all our children were devastated with their dad's death, I think Tommy took it hardest because he had been so involved in his dad's care. When he went home after the funeral, he had multiple troubles on top of his grieving and he chose to go off by himself to get his life back in control. I understand that. He is my son, and I was a psychiatric nurse, two gifts that help me realize the issues and devastation of emotional upsets.

What brought Tommy back to me? His son. He became a daddy during his separation from us, and he wanted me to meet my grandson. I wanted him to meet my new husband. With their similarities, Weldon and Tommy get along well. Both of them are electricians, they both love to fish, and they like sports. Tommy is a good daddy and very proud of his little boy. He and little Thomas visit us often and that little boy keeps Weldon and me entertained. If you ask his name, he rattles off the whole thing, "Thomas Edward Baurys, the third." He knows that his grandpa, who was the first Thomas Edward Baurys, is in Heaven with God. Little Thomas is the only grandchild that we see often, and I miss my other grandchildren but most of them are in their teens or older now, they have busy lives. I can live with that, as long as we keep in touch as well as we can.

Shortly after he came back into my life, Tommy and his significant other got married in a beautiful ceremony, which Weldon and I attended. Unfortunately, after a short time together his wife decided she didn't want to be married so she filed for divorce. Now he is going through the same agonies of getting legalities settled through the court system that his brother Jeff went through several years ago. This is the fourth time for me to offer support and heartfelt prayers for one of our offspring who is enduring the pains of divorce. It doesn't get any easier. I agonize too.

My Ditto Daughters group was important in my journey, too. However, the original group fell apart for awhile. Janie's husband retired from the ministry and they moved to another town. Sherry's work-schedule changed and she could no longer make it to our gatherings. The last I heard of Donna, she had picked up more clients which kept her busy. I missed a lot of meetings after Weldon came into my life because we often had other plans on Monday evenings, so I dropped out of the group. Dee and Dana left our church and became members in other congregations so I don't see them much anymore. I am happy that they eventually found new partners to get the group going again. When I needed human contact for support, God had connected me with this group of dear Christian sisters, and I was deeply nourished by their helpful advice, their listening hearts, and their unconditional love. I can't imagine what it would have been like without them during my adjusting period. Even though I am no longer active in the group, I will always think of these women as my special sisters and forever feel a connection to them.

I could not wrap up this summary of my journey without mentioning Weldon. Have I ever regretted accepting God's gift of another spouse so late in life? No way! Now in our sixth year of marriage, our time together has been one of utter joy. Weldon is not only a caring, romantic husband, but he's my best friend. When I feel like crying, he's the one I turn to. When I have something to laugh about or a good joke to tell, I can't wait to share it with him. When my soul stirs with the presence of Christ in one of life's

Godly moments, I am glad Weldon is at my side. When I need advice or help with something, he's the one whose counsel I trust.

Oddly, we were married awhile before I realized how much he is like my dad, who was a hero to me. Dad was quiet and soft-spoken, a hard worker, generous, compassionate about other people's troubles, and he loved children. He died in an accident when I was seventeen. He didn't see me graduate from high school, he wasn't there to walk me down the aisle when I married, and he never saw my children. Now in my seventies, I still miss having him to talk to, but God sent me someone just like Daddy, and with the same wonderful qualities. Weldon is my hero now. In addition to all his good qualities, he has had a positive effect on my spiritual life, too. I no longer live two lives, my secular and spiritual parts have been pulled together; I am whole.

Since Weldon retired, we've spent all our time together. We traded our little bass fishing boat for a pontoon boat and I love going out to a lake to spend long days afloat, listening to music, dangling our poles in the water, and watching the sunset. We like being out in nature, away from interruptions. People often ask if we get bored with each other's company or if we get annoyed with one another. The question comes mostly from other oldsters who are thinking of retiring themselves and afraid of how it will affect their lives. We always encourage them to go for it. As Weldon says, "We can always find something to do."

Every night before going to sleep, he kisses me and tells me he loves me. I tell him that I love him more. The words need to be said. There won't be a time when we regret not saying them. Often I awake in the early morning hours when the world outside our window is still dark and silent, and the only sound I hear is the hushed rhythm of Weldon's breathing. Without stirring, I'll raise my eyelids and peek across the pillow to see if he is awake. He doesn't open his eyes, but sometimes he smiles like he knows I'm looking at him and he's glad I'm there beside him. I'm glad, too. I close my eyes again and send a silent "thank you" heavenward—several times, because once isn't enough for how I feel.

Weldon is the reason God brought me to Waxahachie.

At our age, many of our friends are celebrating their 50th and 60th wedding anniversaries. We know we'll never live long enough to do that, but every day together is a celebration for us. If anyone were to ask me what I thought was the secret for a good marriage, I'd say two things: first, make sure God is involved in selecting your mate, and second, be sure you can be good friends as well as lovers.

I had no idea that God's new plan for my life would involve another partner. Looking back to my beginnings, I believe it was His will all along. When I was born in Pennsylvania and Weldon was a toddler in west Texas, God most likely had already predestined us to be together one day—when His timing was right. Think about it. Thousands of miles between us were reduced to a pinpoint where we ended up in the same town, on the same street, and it came to fruition after more than sixty years of living out the individual events in our lives that brought us to this point. Does that give you goose bumps? Make the hair on the back of your neck stand up? It does that to me, but it shouldn't. Though the concept is miraculous and almost too big to comprehend, God already has plans for each of us from the moment we're created. David explains this beautifully while praying to God in Psalm 139: 13, 16: *"For you created my inmost being; you knit me together in my mother's womb....your eyes saw my unformed body. All the days ordained for me were written in your book before one of them came to be."*

What I've shared with you is my story. We all have stories, and they're all different. They may change at times to get us where God needs us to be, in order to work out His plan for us, or to use us to facilitate His plan for others (that's when we become angels to deliver messages for Him). We don't know what He will do, or when. That's why it's so important to listen always, and learn to trust Him with all that we are and all that we will become in the Potter's hands. If I were to die today I'd be okay with it because I've had all I could hope for on earth, and I hope I've done all that was expected of me. I think my most amazing journey will be meeting God face-to-face and exploring the wonder of eternity. That doesn't mean I'm in a rush. Because Weldon and I met so late, we'd like to have as much time together as possible. Weldon said he'd like to live to ninety-seven, the age his beloved grandpa died. I wouldn't mind making it to one hundred, just because that number seems like a special milestone on the highway of life. But no matter when we go to be with our wonderful, awesome God, I already know how our story will end: They lived happily ever after, in the little town with the funny name beside Interstate Highway 35.

Endnotes

1. John Ruskin quote source – BrainyQuote.com, "John Ruskin Quotes."

2. William Penn quote source – ThinkExist.com, "William Penn Quotes."

3. Candice Bergen quote source – Good Housekeeping Magazine, January 2009 issue, "What I Love About My Age."

Helpful Scriptures for Journeyers

B e strong and courageous. Do not be terrified; do not be discouraged, for the Lord your God will be with you wherever you go.   Joshua 1:9

For he will command his angels concerning you to guard you in all your ways; they will lift you up in their hands, so that you will not strike your foot against a stone.

Psalm 91: 11, 12

And surely I am with you always, to the very end of the ages.   Matthew 28:20

Do you have eyes but fail to see, and ears but fail to hear?

Mark 8:18

He who belongs to God hears what God says. The reason you do not hear is that you do not belong to God.

John 8:47

Come near to God and he will come near to you.

James 4:8

Each one should use whatever gifts he has received to serve others, faithfully administering God's grace in its various forms.

1st Peter 4:10